FOREWORD

Dear Reader,

In the summer of 1990, life as I knew it turned upside down.

As a child born with full access to extrasensory perception, I had caught the attention of a devoutly religious town and with it, a local sociopath who belonged to a cult intent on ridding the world of evil, evil which due to my "mysterious" abilities they mistook in me. Little did I know it but that summer was to determine the next thirteen years of my life.

I lost my entire childhood and reality to repeated ritual torture at the hands of this man (whom I was led to believe was my real father), and the cult he belonged to. For thirteen years and longer, I was entangled in a living nightmare. A nightmare that I see now was my intention for this life. Upon reading this, I know most people may at first balk at the notion of anyone choosing an experience such as the one I lived through, especially given the fact that I quite nearly did not survive it at all.

I survived for this reason...

Despite all the years and all the horrific ways my abusers tried to exorcize my abilities from me, they did not go away.

They did not go away, and neither did the knowledge I came into this life with.

And now, seven years after I got away, I share this knowledge with you.

It is my sincere hope that all you who read this book allow yourselves to unfold and open up to the spiritual aspect of your lives. It is my desire that you know a softer, less tangible part of yourself which is capable of openness, love, compassion, and joy is yours at all moments of the day.

It will never go away, no matter what you do and no matter what is done to you.

May you become eternally intimate with this side of yourself, and may you know the kind of bliss this intimacy brings. May you know your worth, your freedom, and may you know that you are loved every second of every day.

Sincerely,

Teal Swan (The Author)

THE SCULPTOR
☼ IN THE SKY ☼

Teal Swan

authorHOUSE®

AuthorHouse™ LLC
1663 Liberty Drive
Bloomington, IN 47403
www.authorhouse.com
Phone: 1-800-839-8640

Published by AuthorHouse 06/13/2014

ISBN: 978-1-4567-4725-1 (sc)
ISBN: 978-1-4567-4724-4 (hc)
ISBN: 978-1-4567-4723-7 (e)

Library of Congress Control Number: 2011903229

Acknowledgements

This book is dedicated to all the people of earth who care enough to find bliss in their own lives and therefore create it in the world. And to Winter, my wonderful son who was the long awaited catalyst bringing so much beauty, love, and joy into my life.

This book is also dedicated to the following:

To my parents, whose lives were turned upside down the same day that mine was, who have only ever wanted me to be happy and witness my success. It is my wish that you know we all chose into this experience for a reason. You are not responsible for anything that happened to me in the past.

To my brother, Sky, who has become a compassionate and honorable man. Whom I will never forget was both my companion and source of entertainment at our tiny cabin which had no electricity or indoor plumbing. There is much of playing there with you that I miss.

To my life long friend, Lauren Stokes who has remained as loyal and dedicated to me as she was from the minute we met as children, who had the strength and love enough to stay connected to me through it all. You are perfect to me.

To Blake Dyer, my long lost "brother from a different father and mother" who was the one that hid me when I got away and still provides me permanent sanctuary to this day. You are the kindest person I have ever known.

And finally, this book is dedicated to the man who "ruined" my life. I find in retrospect you did not ruin it at all. I see now that we are only ever victims of victims. I am sorry for the pain I know you suffered in your life. I have stopped the cycle, and now I have you to thank because you were my greatest teacher (as difficulty always is). Without you, I would not have even thought to look for the happiness I now possess today. One day you will know that you are free.

Thanks you and I love you all!

CHAPTER 1
IN THE BEGINNING

In the beginning, there was light.
The immeasurable, unsurpassed cosmos
was a blank fabric of space-time
ready to be woven full of meaning.
Waiting for you.
The history of this universe is woven as easily as silk
from moment to moment as you live it.
And when we trace the thread, back to the beginning
we find that what we really are
is immeasurable-
unsurpassed.

In the beginning there was light. It is the beginning of the story of our universe that nearly everyone has heard. Yet mankind moves through life on Planet Earth year by year and still the same inevitable questions arise.

Who made the light?

Was it God?

Was it the byproduct of an ancient cosmic event within the universe science has been seeking for years?

Why was there light?

For some, the pursuit of answers to these questions is a lifelong devotion. Perhaps this is the reason you are reading this book today. Whatever the reason, you ultimately find yourself opening your experience to the pages you are about to read. It is a promise that the answers you are looking for are already yours. The path you are looking for is a path you are already on- and it will only get better from here. The answers were already yours to begin with. It is not that I seek to answer these questions from some point of higher perspective that is any more expansive than your own, but rather I seek to refresh and reconnect you with your own knowing. And so I ask you to be willing to follow me on a journey of rediscovery of the universe, of God, and of yourself.

Much farther down the road, after this first step within the universe we call "light," you were born.

For quite some time after the moment of your birth, you had full memory of everything that is to follow in this book. That is why upon your birth, you knew and felt your worth as separate from externals. You had no talent, no ability to operate physically within the world, no wealth, and no language. You had no great achievements by society's standards- yet you had infinite worth that you felt very deeply because you simply... were. Everyone around you saw this worth, but they called this your potential- in other words, all the unrealized things you would do, become, and have at a later date. They called this potential- what you would do, become, and have- because they, as adults, had long since forgotten what you still remembered then. What you remembered is this- you cannot ever lose worth or gain worth, because your worth is separate from externals. It is even separate from this life. You were born complete, but not yet completed. You knew then that worth is in the *potential energy* that you are and that the universe is. Within potential energy already exists every yet-unrealized attribute that the adults in your life confused with worth. In fact, worth exists if you do nothing other than breathe and think for the whole of your life. And this potential energy existed before you made the decision to participate in this physical reality you now lead. It exists as you draw your first breath and as you draw your last breath. It exists after you make the decision to no longer participate in this physical life you now lead.

You knew then what your purpose was. It is the same for all of us- living and non-living and that is to be exactly where you are. To do exactly what you are doing in this moment. You knew that growth was inevitable because of this. You knew that you did not become physical so you could find something to put forth effort toward. You came into this physical place to conceive ideas and for those ideas to manifest around you as you let go and allowed them to. You knew then that you did not intend to come here in order to spin in the direction of everything you didn't like about this world and push against it as an attempt to change the world or rid reality of it. You knew your intention to live in the physical was an intention to aid in the full-circle evolution of this universe into a broader and more unified oneness than the oneness that is the underlying eternal truth of this universe. You knew then that this process we are in is the process of one becoming more one, consciousness becoming conscious of itself, God knowing itself, and the separated concept of the self becoming one with God again through the eventual wanting of it. You knew that this life would be the very platform of not only your evolution, but also the evolution of all that is. You knew you did not have to try to do this- it was no sort of quest. You knew then that the way you would do this is to find one single thing in your life, and that is bliss.

The beginning of this journey of rediscovery must start with a limited snapshot of our world today- a snapshot of the current collective, human, and physical reality we have created.

Today, while it is true that the occasional individual finds his or her way to his or her inner truth (the truth of the higher self) and then has full access to bliss, freedom, and awareness- the majority of human society has forgotten that these things are the point of life. Indeed, human society at large has even convinced itself that these things are not based in reality and are therefore instead simply wishful, "Pollyanna" thinking. More importantly, the majority of human society has forgotten that the source of all things is not ever found in events or people outside one's self. It is found within. You may ask then, "What is becoming of this loss of memory of how the universe we live in really operates?" The answer is powerlessness. You can see this every day in the form of war, illness, and fear. Fear sells, illness abounds, and powerlessness finds us as humans in a struggle against everything and everyone- which only brings that 'everything and everyone' we do not want even closer.

In forgetting what it is we came here to do and how one creates reality with focus- human society at large has accepted, individual by individual, a nightmare virus. This is the idea that the individual has no control, freedom, or power. The trend began centuries ago, as soon as men saw spirituality as a means to control others. The birth of organized religion brought the attention away from one's own spiritual essence and focused it on practices of worship, obedience, and doctrine. The history of religion tells you a lot about the history of men and precious little about God. In fact, much of the historical side of religion is a horrific one- full of corruption, misinterpretation, conspiracy, murder, and tyranny. Almost all of the world's conflicts have been caused by those who were supposed to be in the service of God. Writings pertaining to ancient human culture which have no relevance today (some of which were not even meant to be taken literally), were construed to be the eternal word of God. The history of religion exposes people in the human quest for power realizing for themselves that if another man was allowed to realize his own inherent divinity and power, no one could control him. And so they sought to suppress this, warn against it as abomination, and kill those who disagreed all on the name of God. To many, the idea of spirituality has been lost amidst the rubble of organized religion. This is to throw the baby out with the bath water.

It is true that the inherent flaws of religion have caused many to turn their backs on spirituality entirely. It is conversely true that for many, religion has been their anchor and even their hope. For some, religion has been a much-enjoyed system of safety that caused them to not only look for the divine in the first place, but also to not ever wish to look beyond their specific religion. Whichever side of the coin you stand on, the truth is that God is present within every religion in many different forms. God is also present in the absence of religion. God is not about whom or what is right or wrong. God is not about our human-imposed details. God is the essence of the eternal loving omnipresence in all life. God is an essence that is obscured by human rules, doctrine, penance, and righteousness. It is the essence that is always present within every single person, regardless of his or her secular beliefs or what he or she has done in this life.

Religion at its best may be able to make a practice of God. But spirituality is God. It is the thread of love and human divinity that threads similarity through every religion and unites them. From the vantage point of God, the nightmare that makes up much of our religious past is not the big picture. For example, from the perspective of God, even this nightmare many are living currently is pulling them closer and closer to its very opposite. We are slowly pulling ourselves toward love, joy, awareness, and the truth that all living and non-living parts of this universe are intertwined. It is how it was always intended to be.

The reality we live in comes from within. There is no external reality that we participate in to force it into being what we want and force it to be rid of what we don't want. The world is not a space in which we come in order to prove ourselves worthy of something higher. To God, the world we have created is full of beauty. There is not only more beauty than there is ugliness (and all that is restricting you from that view is focus), but it is also the ugliness that is giving rise to this beauty in the first place. To God, worth and bliss are collectively like an inner light that you cannot lose and cannot gain. All the things you think, do, have, and become are built like a stained glass window in front of that light and amplify the beauty of that light, or like cobwebs in front of a window that obscure that light. It is a promise that by the end of this book, you will feel the stirrings of this memory deep within you- and as a result, you will know forever after that it is you who holds the power to decide to get back onto the path you intended. This path is the path of welcoming and becoming your own bliss.

We speak of the beginning because it is a concept that one cannot escape when operating in a three-dimensional reality. We are linear thinkers because this is the dimension in which our physical lives are lived. This means that we are perpetually in search of the beginning of our universe as we know it. This presents a problem when trying to know the truth of the universe at large, because there is no such thing as a true beginning within something that is eternal. Eternal means extending in both the direction of the future and the past, so it is more of a circular concept than it is a linear one. The closer you get to understanding the properties of the most minuscule components of the universe that make up all that is physical- such as atoms, neutrons, electrons, quarks, and leptons- the more apparent the eternality (non-beginning) of the universe becomes. This does not deter us from still searching for a beginning, such as the Big Bang Theory. In doing so, we are missing the big picture as well as the fact that the big picture cannot be complete without the component of God. It is impossible for something to be created (and therefore appear at random, incidentally) from nothing.

All things, including our universe, are the result of what has been previous to those very things. This universe always *has been* and always *will be*, regardless of whether it is manifested in a three-dimensional capacity or not. It is eternal and therefore, it undergoes no beginning or end- but rather, it endures profound cycles. The state of the universe we are living in is a continuation of the state of the universe that was before it. To science, the universe appears to be expanding. This is purely because as multi-dimensional energy increases and changes, it appears in the three-dimensional reality to disestablish the position of physical things. Therefore, as the space between those newly moved things is measured and called distance, the conclusion is drawn that the universe is expanding in size, when this is not the case at all. The universe is not expanding in size- it is expanding in energy, and as such, new dimensions are coming to be. As these new dimensions are coming to be within this universe (which are, at this point, completely invisible to three-dimensional perception as well as measuring devices), it appears to us as if there is a new kind of energy that is increasing called dark matter.

When a new collective evolution within the universe happens, the universe must become greater to compensate for that new idea. To do so, instead of increasing in size, it undergoes a sort of division- like the way the cells of your body divide. However, when the universe divides, it divides in terms of dimensions. When a dimensional division occurs, quite often in the third dimensional reality, it causes the appearance of what we may call an implosion or explosion. Then everything about the reality of that dimension changes in its nature, properties, and laws. This physical effect caused by expanding dimensions that we experience in the third dimension as an explosion is the reason for the birth of the Big Bang Theory. It is, however, just a snapshot in a perpetual universal evolution. Each new dimension has a higher energetic vibration than the last. Within each separate galaxy of this universe, you will find much evidence of the multiple dimensions inherent in our universe, such as black holes. These black holes not only pull energy, as is popularly thought, but they also emit it. They are interdimensional portals. They do not abide by the same properties as objects in the third dimension because of their interdimensional nature. This is why they distort space-time, among other things. They cannot be scientifically understood by us in the current format that we use, because they are on an entirely different energetic vibration than what we can access from the energetic vibration of this third dimensional reality. The unitarity of black holes, for example, is also the result of the fact that they are interdimensional in nature. Dark matter and black holes are not negative space, but are simply the experience of interdimensionality within the universe.

To understand the nature of this universe, however, we must go back even further- past what science has called the Big Bang of our current physical reality and past the beginning of all dimensions. Though eternality is not linear, for the sake of communication, we can call this the beginning of the beginning. At this point, all was one. This concept of oneness is a concept that from our physical brain's point of view, we cannot conceive of as more than a deep knowing, perhaps in the form of a feeling. This oneness existed in a state of potential energy. It was everything and it's opposite. This oneness had a unifying consciousness. To even put a name on that which is unquantifiable, eternal, and limitless is to immediately make this unified consciousness an 'it' and therefore lose the true nature of it. However, for the sake of communicating these things to you hereafter and as a stepping stone to your own personal knowledge of this consciousness, you should know that this consciousness has gone by many names in human society- some of which you may be familiar with: the Great Spirit, Adi Purush, energy, Numen, Almighty, the immense ultimate, the omniscient, the unified field, Allah, the higher self, or God. I will refer to this oneness, however, as Source throughout this book, since it is a neutral word that captures at least a bit of the essence of this unified consciousness. Before you are born into this physical experience, you exist in and as the space of being of Source. Though it can be said that you have a certain sense of self, it is not the kind of sense of self that imbues a differentiation or separation from anything else in your objective awareness. You exist in essence as what can be called your higher self. Your higher self is the eternal, incorporeal, omnipotent, consciousness which is your real self. It is the being that you go forth from and withdraw back to from life to life. It is the summation of all that you have ever been and all that you are. It is often called a higher self because the frequency of the energetic vibration of Source, and therefore your higher self could be interpreted as a much higher frequency than that of physical structure. Your connection to your higher self is unbreakable. It is in fact the focus of your higher self into the idea of you that created you in the first place. Your higher self is not a unit of energy so much as it is a smaller current within the larger current of source.

Long ago, this unified consciousness we will call Source had its first desire- to know itself. And to know itself, the state of oneness could only happen from the platform of separateness. Within this oneness came the first deviation from oneness- the first movement- the first contrasting energetic vibration that did not resonate with the rest in this non-place that was still only non-physical at that point. The more movement attracted movement, the more separate it became. Physical reality is as separate as it gets.

The first manifestation of the physical that came from that process of separation was light. Light is purely a form of electromagnetic radiation. We call this electromagnetic radiation the first manifestation because it had a very important property that had not existed up until that point in its dual nature- it not only had wave-like properties, but also particle-like properties. Particles are, in essence, energetic vibrations that appear to be static, unchanging, and finite. The properties and behaviors of the particle are the reason this physical reality appears static and feels real to you. Everything you see, feel, and touch is nothing but a specific movement that we could call a vibration of energy that has been moved or vibrated for so long that it has become so separate, it appears static. This physical experience appears static to you, but it isn't. Your ears, eyes, nose, tongue, and nervous system (which are also vibrations of energy) are simply interpreting other energetic vibrations, and those energetic vibrations are what you experience as sight, taste, smell, touch, and sound. The idea that the physical is all there is, and that physical structure is static, unchanging, and non-mutable is one of the biggest illusions there is. We are in a time you could call the time of awakening or the new age. We have reached a point where we are coming back toward Source, or knowing oneness. Each generation born now is more aware and less able to become disconnected from their inner knowledge of Source. Times- which are always changing- are changing at an even faster rate.

It may seem odd to many of us that this unified consciousness would want to leave oneness in the first place if it already had it. But it is, in essence, a very cosmic, expansive form of what T.S. Elliot wrote: "We shall not cease from exploration and the end of all our exploring will be to arrive where we started and know the place for the first time."

Source is, at its core, the role of being. Secondary only to this being, however, is its role as creator- the role we are concerned with in this physical reality. As such, in order to fulfill the desire to know itself and true oneness, a law was created within the universe that would supersede all physical laws we experience today. The word law, as it applies to this original desire, simply means a universal property that is binding, recurring, unanimous, and fundamental to the nature of the universe. It was the "law of oneness." In this time and age, this law has been called by many the "law of attraction," so for continuity's sake, I will stick with this terminology hereafter. The law of attraction could accurately be called the law of oneness, because Source knew that this law was a full-circle law, meaning that due to its nature, it would serve to separate Source to its furthest extent, only to then catalyze all separateness back to true oneness. Simply put, the first deviating energetic vibration from this oneness drew other energetic vibrations to match it from the oneness, and each deviation drew more deviation until deviation had reached its furthest point. Once it reached this point, the law of attraction, in continuing to draw energetic vibrations together (like to like), began to draw these separated energetic vibrations back to oneness.

The law of attraction boils down to this: that which is like unto itself is drawn.

On the most expansive level, if there is not such a thing as something that is not Source, and like attracts like, then ultimately there is no other truth and no other end result than oneness that could ever be had.

You could think of the law of attraction as the directing force of all energetic vibration within the universe. It is directing the energetic vibrations that are a resonating match together and directing the energetic vibrations that are not a resonating match away from each other on the level of spirit, thought, and physical reality alike. There is no pause button to the law of attraction; there is no loophole. It is working day in and day out eternally. When we as humans are not aware of the true freedom we have, we do not tend to like the idea of a law- but let it be known (as will be explained in-depth later on in this book) that this law can be your very best friend. Even though it is working, whether or not you understand it, you do not have to understand it *perfectly* in order for it to work. Once you do truly understand it, you will not wish at any point to be free of it.

CHAPTER 2
WHAT AM I AND
WHY AM I HERE?

I am here.
A hand,
a foot,
a face-
to witness the arrivals and departures of each season of my life
as each climbs to its pinnacle
only to slip into the consumptive reach of time.
An intricacy of manhood
in perpetual search of the divine.
But why?

One of the energetic vibrations that deviated from Source was the energetic vibration of thought. This is what created the current we call your higher self. From the energetic vibration of thought came the energetic vibration of Tulpa (that which some cultures call thought form), and from the energetic vibration of Tulpa came the energetic vibration of physical form. You are such a physical form. Essentially, you are a thought that Source and ultimately your higher self thought into being. As such, you- sitting here reading this today- are like the farthest reaching development of Source. You cannot be separate from it. You are it. Though as you are living your life as a pioneer portion of Source, and therefore your higher self, you often forget that you are much more expansive than this physical form. You are the "you" that you know exists simultaneously on *all* these previously mentioned levels. You have also forgotten that as this pioneer portion of Source energy, the very evolution of Source itself is happening because of you.

Projecting oneself into this static and particle-like dimension called the physical (from the standpoint of the non-physical) part of you is not only a noble decision, but also an enthusiastic one. The physical, due to its nature, has a way of inspiring evolution in the universe in a way no other dimension can. It does this by becoming the tangible manifestation of whatever it is that you are energetically vibrating. To Source, this means that physical reality is a very definitive playground of opposites- good and bad, positive and negative alike. This defined way of experiencing what it is that you are resonating with helps you- and therefore Source- know what you want. It is through this focus on what you want that Source knows not only what to become, but also what it is.

Every time you experience something you see as negative, you give rise to its opposite within you. It is only in the presence of black that we can know that which we call white. It is only in the presence of that which we call negative that we can know positive. This playground of opposites is causing you- day in and day out- to come to ideas of improvement, and it is these improved and amended ideas that Source becomes. The evolution of Source to become these things is immediate. The moment you give rise to a positively amended idea, that idea- which now exists as an energetic thought vibration- is what your higher self becomes the exact energetic vibration of. It becomes this improved idea. It becomes this amended energetic vibration. But you are still this pioneer portion of your higher self- and as such, you are able to hold a different energetic vibration from the energetic vibration that your higher self and Source at large holds (and therefore *is*) because of you.

This is an unnatural state, however, and you will know this because when you are resonating at a different frequency than that which you have created, it comes through to you by way of you feeling bad emotionally. You hold this opposing resonance to your higher self and to what you want because you are still thinking thoughts that are vibrating at the frequency of the previous idea instead of the frequency of the amended, improved idea. You are thinking these thoughts with enough regularity that they have become either conscious or subconscious beliefs. In this physical reality it feels often like beliefs are static truths, but they are only thoughts that are thought so often that they are yielding more thoughts exactly like them due to the law of attraction. When these thoughts begin to yield physical and tangible manifestations, you then call it proof. This "proof" then reinforces the belief you started out with and from there, you are caught by default in this snowballing cycle of being out of control over your own energetic vibration.

You are caught in this cycle because you have lost the most valuable knowledge of all—the knowledge that it is you, and *only* you who controls your thoughts.

This is powerful knowledge because your thoughts control your resonance, and your emotions will tell you if you have chosen the right thought and therefore are resonating with negative (not in tune with what you want to create) or positive (in tune with what you want to create) vibration. Most people are caught in a cycle of creating by default, meaning they may be unaware of what they are resonating with because they do not understand what their emotions mean, and so they are not aware that they control their own thoughts. Instead, many people are caught in a state of thinking that their thoughts and feelings come in response to the things that are happening to them- when the truth is exactly the opposite. To get caught in this default system of living is to be stuck in a state of only noticing manifestation and missing the precursor to manifestation, which is the entire truth of life. The truth is that anything that is *in* your life is *a result* of what you were previously resonating with. To know this and then learn how to use this knowledge to be the conscious creator of your life is to live in a state of pre-manifestation comprehension, which was your plan for coming into this life in the first place.

Before you thought yourself into physical form, you had no fear of being on a playground where negative vibrations of energy and their manifestations exist. You knew it did not have to serve as anything more than an aid in helping you define who to become. In other words, you knew it would help you define your bliss. You were in a space where you had not forgotten the ultimate freedom you were- and knowing you controlled your thoughts completely, you were not afraid that you would adopt these negative vibrations and find energetic resonance with them. Instead, the physical dimension looked like an exalted version of a candy store where you could observe and experience- and through observing and experiencing the flavors and textures of what you liked and disliked, you could better know what it was you wanted. By turning your focus to what you wanted, you would then have it. You knew you wouldn't even have to look for it, because in this candy store called physical life anything you can conceive of is yours due to the law of attraction. It is brought to you with absolutely no effort at all. The "how" of it is not your job, and it never was your job. You knew before coming into physical expression that this dance of using negativity as the platform for becoming positive could not only be enjoyable and beneficial to you, but also that it would benefit all that is. When you find bliss knowing that the ultimate truth to the universe is the truth of oneness, all find bliss along with you.

Before you came into this physical being, you watched your parents with full knowledge of their life experience and you made the decision to come into physical expression with them based not only on their positive energetic vibrations, but also on their negative ones. You understood then what those energetic vibrations would help you become. Your intentions for your life (as well as theirs) may have in fact been so strong that you made the plan with them to come into the same physical experience together before they had even become physical themselves. It may not feel like it right now, but the experience of the negative is far more beneficial to you than it is detrimental. You could not evolve if you had nothing to evolve away from. There would be no movement within the universe if everything in your experience was only positive. You would not give rise to a single idea, and therefore, you could not create. There would be no free will in that, and the ultimate truth of your existence is that you are free. That would be the end, and we are not there.

The thoughts giving rise to the physical reality humans experience today have evolved so far as to have reached the idea of the process of birth (both the negative and positive of it) for many beneficial reasons. However, for birth to happen, a baby must be small enough to fit through a woman's birth canal- and as such, a human baby is born nearly premature comparatively. Therefore, it needs a great deal of physical care. The mistake we make is in looking at the baby and saying, "I am this baby's caretaker, I am this baby's provider, I am this baby's safety, I am this baby's guidance"- and it is obvious to us because the baby appears to be so feeble. That baby, who has a very divine purpose and was being guided and energetically fed into being by its higher self for the first nine months with no effort was not abandoned to its parents upon the moment of birth. This stream of Source continues for its entire life.

The instinct to care for a newborn is energy from Source flowing through a parent, inspiring them to do so. It feels like a positive compulsion to do so. Where we start to get into trouble is when we try to take over for the Source energy that is this child and override the infant with our own energetic vibrations and our idea that life means struggle and that this baby is ours instead of being one of us who has merely come into the physical at a different time than we did.

Life does not have to mean struggle if we are not in the vibrational state of resistance to our higher selves. When as parents, we have forgotten that we are conscious creators of our experience. Instead we live in fear, thinking that it is possible for others to do anything they want to us. We look at our infant and immediately start demonstrating the backward art of pushing ourselves against this Source flow that we each have within us. We immediately begin to teach, verbally and nonverbally, that the way to achieve happiness is to control the manifestations around us, otherwise known as external physical reality. We do this malediction by our example, which is the greatest, if not the only way there is to truly teach. But gaining happiness by controlling the external manifestations we have already thought into being is an impossible quest. Most people in society care much more about a child finding a way to please them through its actions than a child finding a way to please itself through its thoughts and then subsequent inspired actions. This is because most people have not found a way back to their own happiness yet, so the cycle continues like that from generation to generation.

A parent begins by saying, "This baby belongs to me and must behave in a certain way for me to be happy." While this is not a concept that a baby agrees with, at some point in childhood (because this eternal being is new to the practice of physical life and practices it by mimicking what it sees around it), the child is influenced enough to decide to adopt these imposed behaviors and therefore begins to find resonance with them. The child becomes more motivated by the approval or disapproval directed at him or her by others than his or her own higher self or emotions. In time then, the child is guided away from his or her own internal knowledge. The child starts to think his or her self-worth is based on what he or she does and how well he or she does it. Worth subsequently becomes obscured. It is not relinquished or gone, but the child and subsequent adult has lost sight of it.

It is a decision we make to conform to our environment in this way when we are born because in most cases, we decide it is more beneficial for us to do so than it is to deal with the potential wrath of not doing so. The decision-while still a decision- can be so subconscious that it does not feel as though it was a choice at all. We forget how to follow our own energy pull, calling, knowledge, and purpose. Though no gone, they are lost from our awareness. This is what happened to our parents as a result of their environment- and to their parents as a result of their environment, and so on and so forth- much farther than you could ever trace. This pattern, however, has given rise to a new collective desire. It is the platform of this negative energetic vibration that is allowing the birth of new generations coming in (and continuing to come in) with the purpose of not forgetting the higher self. The people of these generations will not conform and will not forget. And with them, the rest of society will follow into remembrance.

It is not something that gives most people comfort to understand, though the truth is that it is always a choice to adopt any energetic vibration. Your essence cannot be harmed or lost. No matter what childhood or past you have had, not even the most traumatic experience you could ever conjure into reality could damage your higher self. It will always remain intact and will eternally search for ways to manifest its complete self. The most you can ever do is prevent the energetic flow of the energy of your complete, interminable higher self through your three-dimensional self.

There is not some magic age at which a child suddenly is in control of his or her energetic vibration, has free will, and is subject to laws of attraction. A child- often before it even has capacity for language- chooses to assume a negative energetic vibration (such as one of fear) because he or she mimics his or her parents' thoughts and way of living. A child's parents have the dominant energetic vibration within the household. This dominant energetic vibration- being very influential, as dominant vibrations are- is the energetic vibration that the child's attention is focused upon. It is not the child's fault- he or she is merely in such a mode of observance during the adjustment into physical existence that he or she assumes this energetic vibration by default. Despite this lack of awareness that leads to default adoption of negative energetic vibrations, the truth is that it is ultimately a choice to do so. It is for this reason that it was a choice in the first place- and you can, at any point in your life, no matter how ingrained and practiced your negative energetic vibrations are- choose to adopt and therefore resonate with a different vibration.

So how do you know whether you are holding a positive energetic vibration or not? And how do you change your energetic vibration if you are indeed holding a negative energetic vibration?

CHAPTER 3
THE NORTH STAR
CALLED EMOTION

Emotion...
the compass displaying
which path of a thousand paths you are headed down,
between the South of tragedy and the North of bliss.
An internal, lusty, chemical kind of North Star
you can follow all the way home.
Home to Source, straight to the way you want your life to be.

The Law of Attraction is working on every dimension in this universe, including that of Source. Your higher self, and therefore Source, has the ability to switch vibrations immediately, which introduces a vibration of such magnitude that when Source has adopted this identical energetic vibration to the energetic vibration of your amended and improved ideas, just like a magnet, you will begin to be pulled in that direction until you are one and the same. You will be *pulled* (as if magnetically) to opportunities, people, items, and ideas- indeed, toward anything that is an energetic vibrational match to the source of vibration of which your higher self now *is*. Because you are Source, there is no greater likeness in the universe than that of your higher self and you. The universe will be leading you toward your higher self, day in and day out, every moment of your life. You will never be lost. Being inspired by physical life makes want inevitable. And so- growth, betterment, and evolution are inevitable byproducts of physical life- no matter what you do.

If you walk the path of nonresistance- if you let go and just let yourself be pulled magnetically by your higher self (which is acting in your best interest at all times) - your life will be blissful and you will get every single thing you want. You are always a match to that which your higher self is. But you can despite this by thinking thoughts that resonate with negative energetic vibration in opposition to your higher self. If you were not able to hold a separate vibration than your higher self, you could not experience enough to even identify your wants, and Source could not evolve. There would not be any disparity to want or learn from. When you do this, however, it is as if you are half of the magnet that has now reversed itself in that you are causing incredible vibrational friction in a form of battle that you cannot ever win. When you do that, you are restricting the circulation of your higher self's focus through you- and you will lose energy. Eventually, your physical body will deteriorate- on top of the fact that you will now be a match to the manifestation of anything that matches your current negative vibration. You need not fear this, because you will know if you are doing this based on how you feel. This is never intentional- but if you are feeling any negative emotion, this is what you are doing.

Most people moving through this physical dimension as adults today have forgotten their most acute and accurate sense of all- emotion. Most people are aware emotions exist but view them as a menace- something to fight, something they are powerless to, a drawback, or even something to distrust. The average person does not know what emotions are and does not know why emotions are. We are in a tug of war between being a slave to them and flipping around to wage war on them. We have a multi-billion dollar pharmaceutical industry set up to profit from chemically aiding people to suppress their emotions and change them externally. All of this is resistant to Source, to our true selves, and to the true bliss that is possible at any moment from wherever you are, because *all* of your power is in the now. Your emotions are the compass guiding you through this venture called life. They are all the guidance you will ever need.

You are a specific energetic vibration made up of a collection of energetic vibrations- all of which are under your control. Source does not view the negative energetic vibrations in thought or in the physical as negative, because they serve a divine purpose. Source itself is undiluted, positive energy. It is this way because we desire it to be. Source becomes the vibration of whatever we have *truly* wanted. I use the word truly with regards to our wanting because Source has a better idea of what we truly want than we at times even have conscious awareness of. Source knows, for example, that no one truly wants to kill another person- what people who kill want is to feel in control of themselves and their reality in efforts to feel free. Killing someone is just an impulsive, immediate attempt some make to gain back freedom and a sense of control from their current position of powerlessness, insecurity, and fear. This is why Source is entirely benevolent.

The moment you hold a thought, it is either in resonance with what you want- the energetic vibration of your higher self and how Source sees something you are giving focus to- or it is in discord with what you want. You could think of this like an energetic symphony. When you give your attention to a subject, the thoughts you are thinking about that subject have an energetic vibration that could be compared to a musical note or frequency. That frequency either matches the frequency of the orchestra at large (called Source), or it does not. If it does not, you are disallowing the flow of music (the flow of energy from your higher self) to flow. When you disallow this flow, you are disallowing yourself from becoming a match to what you desire. And so, you are disallowing joy and you are disallowing freedom.

Moving on with this analogy of music, just as there are the musical notes of *a, b, c, d, e, f,* and *g,* there is no musical note that represents the equivalent of "not *a*" or "not *b*." There is no "anti-vibration" within the universe. You are either in energetic resonance with what you want, or you are in resonance with something else. If you focus on the idea of "I don't want A," or "not A," then your resonance will be with none other than... A. For example, if you know you don't want A, then the only way to use the Law of Attraction to your benefit is to find out that by knowing you don't want A, you therefore want B, and then choose to focus on (and therefore find resonance with) B.

The way to know if you are in resonance or discord with what you want- and with your higher self- is to gauge how you feel. Your emotions are the conductor of this symphony of energetic vibrations. Most of you have heard a musical note that is out of tune and most of you have heard a musical note that is in tune. Your negative emotions are what happen when you are out of tune, and your positive emotions are what happen when you are in tune. These energetic vibrations manifest themselves physically in the form of neuro-peptides that cause an electrical charge to the neurons in your brain that compel you in one way or another. You could say, in effect, that emotions are physical, chemical manifestations of the energetic vibration of the thought you are thinking at any given moment.

But you are more than your brain, and thus you should never confuse the mind with the brain. The brain is simply a sophisticated, flesh-composed computer of energetic vibrations. Thought, what you could call "the mind," exists beyond the brain, meaning it is not the brain that gives rise to thought but rather thought that gives rise to the brain. The brain enables you to interact with the physical, and when the brain is damaged, this is the only task you can no longer perform. If you think of these energetic vibrations of thought as musical notes, the path from the furthest note from your higher self to the note of being in perfect resonance with your higher self, as you can imagine, encompasses a wide range of notes in between. Each of your emotions accounts for one note between these two extremes- bliss and freedom being on one end of the line, and total powerlessness and fear being on the other end of the line. Your emotions are telling you at every moment, like a compass, if what you are thinking and living is correct or incorrect for you.

Instead of distrusting emotion, we should embrace it wholeheartedly as the completely reliable, consistent compass that guides us through our lives- because this is what emotion is. It is only when we ignore this emotional compass that we become convinced that emotions have ever failed us and are ever negative in nature. In effect, we ignore our internal compass while this guidance is screaming at us louder and louder, and then we blame our compass for the reason that we are upset because it feels so unnatural and miserable to be going in the wrong direction. Emotions are only the gauge informing us of what we are thinking at any moment. We have the ability whenever we feel that negative emotion to do one thing- and that is to find a thought that more closely resonates with the frequency of Source. We will know it more closely resonates because the thought will make us feel better.

There is no right or wrong to this. People sometimes do not recognize when they are getting closer to finding resonance with their wants (their higher self) because the energetic vibration of anger is actually closer to resonance with the higher self than fear or sadness is. What will feel better to someone in the space of fear or sadness is thinking a thought that feels like anger. The energetic vibration of pessimism is closer to resonance with the higher self than the energetic vibration of anger, so what feels better than a thought of anger is a thought that feels like pessimism. What feels better than a thought of pessimism is a thought of optimism, and what feels better than a thought of optimism is a thought that feels like happiness. Once you have reached that, you are resonating with your higher self. Do not condemn your (or someone else's) anger- ever. If it comes after a feeling of fear or sadness, it is a serious improvement. Once your anger becomes the bad-feeling place, look for a thought that makes you feel better than anger does- and so on and so forth. You can do this with your innate gift of focus.

You have control of your focus. Focus on the most important aspect of creating your life. It is a skill that takes practice- and practice is nothing more than repetition. When you find a thought that feels better than the thought you are currently thinking, the Law of Attraction will magnetically bring you another good thought- and then another, and then another. Whatever energetic vibration or thought you are holding is subject- like everything is subject- to the Law of Attraction. Therefore, things in your physical realm will reflect perfectly back to you what energetic vibration you hold. The physical life that you identify with is a perfect reflection of your most practiced energetic vibrations, or thoughts. If you begin today to practice focusing on thinking thoughts that make you feel better, you will begin to follow your emotional navigator into bliss- and the entire world around you that you once thought was an external reality will shift to become the manifestation of that which you have consistently, even unconsciously, defined as your bliss.

Often people are confused about just how important their emotions are. One could accurately say that emotion is the most important thing in this universe, because all emotion exists to reflect to you whether you are in resonance with your higher self (and therefore Source itself) or in discord with it.

At all moments there are two ways of moving to find resonance with your higher self, or bliss itself. The first is to realize that you are a manifestation of the energy of your higher self which is direct Source energy, which becomes what we want the second we want it- so anything you want, you already have. The second is to want the *now*. Anytime you find appreciation for what already is, you want it. And when you want what is, you have instantly attained resonance with your higher self. You will feel Blissful. Neither of these techniques is better or worse than the other. They are, in fact, incredibly effective if used together. Although, one of the quickest ways to become chronically unhappy is to try to suppress a desire or to try to look at what you don't like about the now and try to force yourself to like it.

There are many belief systems that preach the idea that the correct road in life and the only road to bliss is to rid oneself of desire itself. It is easy to see how it would be a quick assumption to make that unhappiness comes from not getting something you want, therefore causing you to live in a perpetual state of "the grass is greener on the other side." If you lived in this kind of reality, it would seem to you that the root of evil and what brings unhappiness in the first place is desire. But this is not the case. This is to throw the baby out with the bathwater. Wanting is not the root of evil. It is the way that the universe becomes more aware of itself. It is the very root of our evolution. It is easy to make it the root of evil if one is not aware that he or she can manifest what he or she desires at any point. It is also easy to make it the root of evil if a person is focused on the world as if it exists outside himself or herself. If you have become convinced that the world exists outside of yourself, you are viewing the world in a finite way where there is the illusion of limit with regards to resources. From that vantage point, it appears that it is possible to take things away from someone. This is a concept we call greed, which entails suffering. Greed does not exist if a person sees this universe as it really is. Often people operate within the physical dimension under the false understanding of a finite universe. In the physical state, it is easy to get stuck in the illusion of boundaries and limitations. It is understandable that someone could get caught up in thinking that Source is like a pool that will be used up if everyone is following their bliss and getting what they want. It is also understandable how it is easy to fall into thinking that being happy means you are detracting from someone else's happiness. This is never the case. This universe, Source, is infinite. There is no boundary, no beginning, and no end to it. Everything that is physical is a condensed form of the nonphysical. Therefore, if you think of it and resonate with it, it must come to be.

The only thing that is getting in the way of your thoughts and resonations coming to be, or of you seeing this as possible- is your focus on how they will come to you, which breeds in you the energetic vibration of pessimism or of being overwhelmed. In that resonance, you are disallowing it to *be*. You are not an energetic, vibrational match to what you thought of and wanted in the first place. The *how* of something is not your job. It gets in the way of the physical realization of everything that you want. You do not ever need to know how something you dream up will come to be. It will simply come to be when your thoughts are a perfect match to what it is you dreamed up. This universe is an unlimited resource. There is more than enough for everyone that is to have everything they want at no detriment- but instead, to the benefit- of anything else that is.

We have also been living by a false idea which is that we must be honest about reality- honest about what *is*. That false idea exists because of the false sister idea that reality exists separate of where our focus is (the false notion that it is external). What *is*, is only an indication of what your focus has been on in the past. There is no such thing as a static reality, and there is no such thing as a reality that exists outside of yourself. Looking at what is because you think you must face and accept reality causes intense focus on what is, which only reinforces the energetic vibration of what is. Therefore, all you will be able to manifest into your reality is more of what is. If you are interested in intentionally creating your life and finding bliss, your focus should be aimed at what you like about what is and what it is that you want to be- and in turn, that will end up being your reality.

CHAPTER 4
DESTINY AND FREE WILL

Of the mystery, the challenge, the gift,
and the illusion of free will-
it can only be said that there is but one opportunity
giving rise to two diverging paths.
On one side, the choice is to use it-
on the other, the choice is to leave it alone.
And either way, you are free.

The argument over the paradox of predetermination and free will is one that has spanned the centuries. This is a paradox because it is not a matter of one or the other being false. The truth lies in the fact that both are simultaneously true. You are playing this life out, and you are also a piece of a bigger picture, which is playing you. The paradox starts with the fact that you are Source- and because of this, you cannot escape the original plan Source had for itself (and therefore you) to evolve. You are fated to evolve, and therein- to think, to feel, and to choose. It is inevitable that whatever you choose will lead Source to the same inevitable state, but it is not predetermined how you will evolve and think and choose. It is your choice of thought and desire in the first place that constitutes free will.

You are Source, so anything you choose is Source's choice. In this respect, the truth of yourself and your existence is complete freedom. But at no point was every minute of every day of your life written before you got here. In a nutshell, truth lies in the fact that you are executing Source's original plan through the free will you execute on a daily basis through your choice of thought. There is no reason to try to rebel against this, because being Source, it was you who made that original plan in the first place. You are not being controlled by anything other than yourself. It just feels that way when you forget that you are Source.

When people traditionally think of destiny, they think of someone laying out all the plans for their lives – someone who is fated to be where they are and do what they are doing. In that realm, the entire plan of people's lives is to be a kind of living chess piece. Destiny is much more complicated than that. When you are not yet focusing thought into the physical form of yourself, you exist as your higher self. You are, in other words, a thought of Source. You are immersed in Source and are intimately one with its far-reaching perspective. It is with this perspective that you continue to ebb and sway in and out of physical form for the purpose of letting physical life help you to become greater. The energetic vibration you hold before being physical becomes a perfect match to the energetic vibrations of everything that you are in the physical dimension. This match is a simultaneous resonance or coming together of your spirit essence, your genes, your personality, your parents, the time and place of your birth, and the entirety of your astrology amongst other things. You knew before you came into this body that the specific energetic vibrations you were about to come into would inspire you to find a way to resonate at the frequency of whatever you should want to resonate with for the purpose of your own vibrational evolution. It is from this perspective that you came in with your overall purpose or intention. On this journey, if you are putting your thoughts into actions that are in line with your energetic purpose, you will feel bliss. This is often the reason behind a person being predisposed toward art, athletics, or any number of things.

When people do things that put them in vibrational resonance with their pre-birth intention, they feel the bliss of that resonance. In the third dimension, we say that it must have been his or her destiny to do that thing. In our resonation with purpose, it feels so right to us to feel the feeling of pre-deliberation that we usually cut ourselves off from the way we live our current physical lives. That being said, we did not lay out all the details of our physical experience before we got here. We began to attract these details once we arrived. Nothing in our lives has to become or will become without our own cooperation. We can alter the course of our lives and our intention at any time. But the intentions of our higher selves are being satisfied by our physical lives and this is why we can often feel destiny in this.

The concept of destiny brings up the subject of reincarnation and karma. Reincarnation is not linear, as you may think, due to the nature of the way your brain works. You reincarnate into a physical dimension because you extend from your higher self and withdraw back to your higher self in an ebb and sway towards physical form and from physical form. Your individual life can be described best with the famous analogy of a candle flame. If you have a flame on a candle, use that flame to light the wick of a different candle, and then blow out the first flame. Is the second flame the same as the first? Or is it different? The answer is that the flame is not the same- and it is also not different. You are not the same from life to life, and you are also not different. Because you are always connected to Source, you have come into this life still connected to what many like to call an "Akashic Record," which is knowledge compiled in the non-physical of all that has been since the beginning. Akashic knowledge is knowledge of oneness, the cosmos, and all human and non-human experience throughout history. It is also knowledge of all your previous lives. This knowledge is encoded in your DNA. You have access to memories of past lives, even if they are not conscious to you.

You have gained understanding in your past lives that has transferred with you into this life, and you will carry it with you into the next life. This standpoint of understanding is responsible for the reason you chose this life. It is also partially responsible for why you show different propensities than others. This knowledge of past lives can be triggered like a distant memory of familiarity by a great many things, such as traveling to a place you have lived in a past life, because even though your opposing energetic vibrations (sufferings) are wiped clean in death so you can have a fresh start, your vibrational slate is not wiped entirely clean from life to life. While it is both hard and not really beneficial to separate what comes from past lives and what comes from this life (like we love to do linearly), memories from past lives can be experienced in our dreams. These memories can be responsible for our unexplainable affinities and interests toward things such as cultures, places, things, our unexplainable talents, and what we innately relate to. It also plays a role in Déjà vu, which is a feeling that can crop up when memories from a past life are triggered. It can also be a feeling that crops up when you definitively know you are on the physical path in life that is in resonance with your higher self and your pre-birth intentions (a crossroads in which you know you have chosen the right place at the right time).

All this being said, it is not reasonable for someone to have a negative holdover from a past life. This is not something that gives people much comfort when they have made past lives the scapegoat of their current problems. So, all of your negativity is negativity you picked up in this life- either by default or deliberately for the purpose of using it for your own evolution. Anyone who is truly capable of seeing your past lives will see them this way also. The only way you can ever accurately and consciously access your past lives (which have been many) is to be at a place where you are completely in resonance with Source- much like the state Buddha reached in his meditation under the Bodhi tree. From that state, they are seen much differently than one would traditionally think. Every thought that has ever been thought still exists. But Source has become only the energetic equivalent of the total positive improvement that has come of those thoughts and experiences of past lives. From the clear state of resonance with Source, you never *feel* intense emotion from something you suffered in a past life, because all that comes from that vantage point is the good that came of it. Your past lives only serve to help you evolve into what you *are*. You are a culmination of all of them. It is for this reason that it is never really helpful, even if it is interesting, to deliberately remember your past lives. If a person thinks he or she sees a negative holdover in you which correlates to a past life, this is really due to the Law of Attraction. This person is picking up on your energetic vibration and seeing the thought images of any past life (not even yours) that corresponds most closely to the negative energetic vibration that you are holding in this life. To complicate things further as per the Law of Attraction, the images are also a match to the person observing them- which means whether they are yours or not, they are an energetic vibrational match to the person seeing the images and calling them yours.

This universe is not a linear one, which means intentions for coming into form can be all over the map. The truth of reincarnation is not in line with the traditional idea that a butcher is then fated to become the animal he has butchered in his next life. There is no cosmic debt you are paying. All of your lives are chosen specifically because of what they will help you evolve into. It may be that when a butcher dies and has re-emerged as his higher self, having evolved into what his life caused him to evolve into, the next step could be that he hopes to gain evolution out of the new perspective that being an animal meeting with a butcher's knife would give him. But you do not attract a life by default based on your last life.

You may, when you have had to die in one life in order to realize your desires, choose to reemerge into a new life with a similar circumstance. You may have the intention of reliving the situation that gave birth to those desires with the intention of realizing those desires before you die in the new life, knowing that the achievement of those desires while you are still living will give rise to an entirely new set of desires- and therefore, a new perspective. Thus, it is easy to interpret this choice as fulfilling unfinished business from one life in the next.

You can, from the standpoint of your higher self, choose to revisit or reactivate the thoughts and thought forms associated with a past life because they still exist. You do not attract a life from the vibration of negativity, because your negative energetic vibration does not follow you past death. This is why it feels good to die. When you die, your thoughts and thought forms are left behind as you withdraw your focus back into the total positive energetic vibration of Source. This is why karma is only a concept of the physical realm. It is the concept that you get what you give- a simplified way of explaining how the Law of Attraction works. Because negative vibration cannot be carried over from life to life, karma does not exist outside the physical dimension. Karma is something people use to justify things over which they think they have no control. It is an attempt to control by trying to scare people into behaving in a way that is beneficial to others. Karma is what people use to explain the manifested aftermath of the Law of Attraction when they are not consciously aware of it.

One could say that death is destiny. It will come to everything that is physical- anything that had a beginning. But in terms of annihilation, death is impossible. There is no such thing as death. It is easy to understand why when we lose our knowledge of the big picture in this life, we would become attached to this singular physical life and say it is all there is. It is easy to view death as a villain when you cannot choose when other people around you will choose to die. It seems that death takes whatever it wants at will. Death causes all people involved to question their own lives and their own eternal natures. But as you are grieving, your grief itself is telling you that you are resonating with your brain and not with your higher self or what your higher self knows about death. It is this discordant energetic vibration that is causing you to suffer.

It is easy to become attached to the physical aspect of this life and say that it is unbearable that when a loved one dies, you cannot touch that person's skin or see him or her physically walking and talking every day. You focus on the absence of them in your scape. But loved ones still exist past death. You can communicate with them. From this standpoint of death, they have more access to you than they ever did in life- because to your higher self, there is no time and place. They can be with you no matter where or when you are. Death is a natural event. In fact, it does not even have to be an event. The reason why you see people suffering greatly during the process of death and declining greatly in health before death has to do with two things. The first is that when people fear and fight against death, they are holding a discordant energetic vibration which gives rise to illness and suffering on many levels of themselves. The second is people's expectations of what will happen before they die. People's beliefs are very dependent on what they see around them in the form of other people (and now on television, in newspapers, and on the internet). An individual may be surrounded by people who do not view death as natural, but fear and fight against death. In that person's flailing against it, he or she declines and suffers, and death becomes a large event instead of the non-event it can be.

This expectation even governs at what age you will die. It is because of your belief- which is based on other people- that no one lives to an age much past the expected old age for their time period. If it was your intention, and you harbored no belief that there was an impending time you are fated to die, you could live for as long as this single life served your interest and the interest of your higher self. That being said, it was never your intention to come into one life- into one point of view- and stay in it for eternity. While that may seem like an alluring idea once you have become attached to the physical aspect of yourself, at some point it would lose its benefit to you, and you would no longer be infatuated with it. The transition into death does not have to be a painful one, and you do not have to decline in health to die unless you believe it will be painful and that you must decline in health to do so.

Death is simply the withdrawal of your higher self's focused energy from the thought of your physical self in this life. While the brain is an amazing tool for physical life if it is used properly, it comes equipped with natural roadblocks from accepting the truth that there is no death. One of these is that it is hard-wired for survival. The brain's purpose is to tell us that we want life. It is hard-wired in this way because that survival instinct serves your higher self in keeping you in the physical long enough that you can benefit from it. This very ingrained chemical pattern, however- like everything else that is- can be changed with your thoughts. The feelings of fear and pain are chemically based and restricted to your physical body. Upon the very moment of death (as most anyone who has had a near-death experience will tell you), your brain and those chemicals that interpret thoughts of fear are left behind. The terrible sensations of pain and fear are left behind with your body, and you will de-manifest.

When you die, you will have the experience of passing into an overwhelming white light. This is because as you reverse this process of manifestation, you will pass through the stage of Tulpa (thought form) and then through the beginning of your physical manifestation, which is light. Because you will be returning to Source, you will be immersed immediately in the undiluted positive energetic vibration of Source. This will feel like heaven to you. It is, in truth, an experience much like the changing of perspectives between being in your physical life and going to sleep in that you emerge into a beautiful feeling dream that is more familiar to you than even your physical life. It is no more dramatic than that transition.

It is also impossible for it to be out of your control to die. You cannot die until the minute that your physical self agrees to do so and therefore resonates with death. Death feels wonderful, no matter who you are or what you have done in your physical life. Even though it is easy to get caught up in a lack of awareness and therefore crave a linear justice of default karma as heaven or hell, there is no punishment or reward waiting for you in the form of a life or place once you die- regardless of what you have done in this life. Heaven and hell are concepts that manifest in the physical dimension. They are right here on Earth. Hell is not a place, but rather a state of mind that becomes the suffering you are living which is being created and drawn to you by the Law of Attraction. It feels terrible because it is the farthest resonance you can find in the opposite direction of resonance with Source. Hell is not a resonance that is compatible with Source, but it is the feeling of being completely unaccompanied by Source or your higher self in the thoughts that you are thinking and the things that you are doing. It is still subject to the Law of Attraction, but you cannot find resonance with Source in that moment.

This may seem like a paradox because you create with your mind, and what you think about is. And so, if so many people are thinking of hell, it is logical that it then must be. However, the entire purpose of physical life and the physical dimension in general is to help Source know itself by becoming exactly what it is we dream up for it to coexist with our wanting. No one wants things that are the vibrational equivalent to negativity. Those vibrations simply exist in the physical dimension (as well as in thoughts coming from the physical dimension) to cause us to clarify and therefore focus on what we want the universe to evolve into. When we die, all there *is* is what we have wanted. When we are alive and living in hell, all there *is* is the focus on what we do not want. Hell is a concept that belongs to those searching for justice from a space of very limited understanding. Hell is what people who try to find security in forcing the external world to be one way or another use in attempt to scare people into good behavior and away from bad behavior.

As long as any negative emotion, such as fear, is the motivation to do (or not to do) something, that motivation does not come from a pure energetic vibration, and therefore, it is not genuine or lasting. The devil is also a character that does not exist. Like hell, the devil is a fictional idea- a thought form that is projected from the mind of people who are physically manifested. It is a concept- like hell- that was invented by the human mind (not Source's mind) as a tool in social and political affairs in order to control others with fear as well as relieve one's self of responsibility. At the time the concept of the devil came about, many leaders sought to gain power through religion. As such, all non-believers, infidels, and heretics (people who were thought to threaten total control) were to be associated with the devil and made to be the enemy of God as well as a threat to the eternal souls of others. This meant immediate condemnation by association for those thought to be in contact with the devil. Even though the association was assumed, it was believed that their souls would go straight to hell. Much like the death penalty, which is still a practice of modern society today- they were put to death under the belief that they would meet with justice in hell and that death is the worst thing that could happen to a person. In all actuality, like everything else that is manifested physically, they simply were put to death only to rejoin the unfiltered, transcendental positive energy and vantage point of Source. In fact, death is a far, far cry from the worst thing that a person can experience. If the majority of people knew that, however, they would most likely stop condemning our most hardened criminals to it.

As you can probably guess by now, heaven-like hell- is also not a place. Heaven is a state of mind that comes from the bliss you are living in your physical life, which is the direct result of your thoughts. Heaven is a state achievable by those who are able to follow the north star of their own emotions so consistently that any resistance to that guidance is not felt within them. While you are living, it is the state of holding the closest energetic resonance to that of Source. It is the feeling you will all have once you die.

CHAPTER 5
BEYOND THE VEIL

May you come to understand that your open eyes deceive you.
What you see is but a fraction of what is.
Beyond the veil of this dimension
you will see that you have never arrived.
You have never departed.
There is no beginning or end to that which is you.

It is a choice one can make at any moment to open oneself to what lies beyond the veil of normal perception. What creates the veil in the first place is the belief that it is there. Over the years, the most attention with regards to the unseen has been dedicated to the subject of ghosts, angels, and guides. There is a debate over whether they exist or not, as well as what they are and what purpose they serve. Let it be known that they do exist. All three are examples of a Tulpa, which is a manifestation of mental energy. People could accurately call this a thought form. A thought form is a thought that has enough energy to become a configuration, shape, or visual appearance. It may manifest in a non-static way or utilize other energetic vibrations to help itself to manifest. The idea of you is a Tulpa in that the essential form of your personality, appearance, likes, and dislikes are who the physical *you is.*

A ghost is an exiting Tulpa. I call it this because it is not a Tulpa that exists because the focused energy of a higher self is now creating it. It is a residual or thought that was once focused. A ghost Tulpa exists when a person leaves their physical body behind and just as that person joins back with their higher self, they leave behind the energetic vibration of the thought of their physical body in relation to this life and the thoughts that did not resonate with the energetic vibration of Source. These types of Tulpas resonate very strongly with the physical dimension, so they often have attachment to a physical object, person, or place by way of resonating with it. These thoughts have enough energy that they can not only assume some version of physical manifestation in the form of an image, but also sometimes in the form of being able to manipulate what is physical, like poltergeist activity. These Tulpas can act out unfinished business in many forms. Though just like a body decays, they tend to lose their energy over time if someone is not lending energy to them by focusing on them.

Ghosts are not people whose souls have become stuck somewhere between life and death. These thought forms, however, can be interacted with and helped to de-manifest. You have most likely heard of a medium helping a ghost cross over into the light. This happens when a medium with a vibrational resonance high enough to interpret the energetic vibration of a Tulpa as a sight or sound offers energetic thought vibrations that influence this thought form to change its energetic vibration and therefore resonate with Source. When it does this, it goes through a process of de-manifestation that retracts it through the primary manifestation stage of light.

This form of an exiting Tulpa is highly dependent on its surroundings to be able to manifest. It can only do so, for example, if the person who died had a lot of energy when they died so the place that person died has inherently a lot of energy, meaning the planets were in certain alignment so as to lend enough energy to the earth itself like during a full moon. The circumstances in which that person died commanded a large amount of energy so living people gave a lot of attention to its existence, or someone around that person was capable of holding a high enough resonance to be able to interact with him or her. Whenever the feeling you get off of a Tulpa is a negative one, you are dealing with the residual thought form of the person and the vibrational state that the person left behind. It is not the person's soul. It does not have direct connection to the Source part of the person who left it behind. The higher self that left it behind does not miss its body or its Tulpa.

If, however, the higher self wanted to have direct connection with its Tulpa again, it could do so by re-resonating with it. If it did this, it would now be an entering Tulpa. It only chooses to do this if it is beneficial. It does this occasionally to attend physical births or deaths of people it was close to in order to aid in the process of death or birth. Occasionally, it will do this to aid a person who is struggling or suffering in life to lend support to them when support would best be lent by the person they were familiar with.

When a portion of Source is in the physical form that goes by your name, your point of view is that of physical form. It means that the vibrational resonance you hold is at a dense enough frequency to make you a physical form. Due to the Law of Attraction, you are an energetic vibrational match to other things that are holding a resonance dense enough to make them physical forms. This is why most people alive today only perceive that which is physical with their five traditional senses. They often perceive what is not physical through their emotions alone, which is the sixth sense. The entire purpose of emotion is to keep the body in touch with its higher self in the nonphysical aspect. Most babies have not entirely taken on a purely physical resonance. They see thought form as well for a time until they train themselves into such resonance with the physical that they lose the frequency that allowed them to see thought forms.

When a person is in the process of death and they withdraw their focus from the energetic vibration of the physical, they will be able to perceive thought form. The person may begin talking to loved ones they once knew because they hold a new resonance which allows them to see their loved ones. Occasionally, a person can grow up with their vibrational frequency maintaining resonance with more than just the physical. In fact, that is the dominant intent of many of the new children being born today. This can happen at birth and be maintained from birth, or it can happen as a result of a near-death experience. It can also be learned. If a person makes it their intention in the life they are living to find an energetic vibration that resonates with thought form, that person can have what you would call clairaudient or clairvoyant experiences. There is no veil between the physical and the non-physical. In truth, there is no distinction between the physical and the non-physical other than the mind of the perceiver.

As for guides and angels, they are true projections of Source into a thought form for a purpose. They are, in a sense, entering Tulpas. Sometimes it is of extreme benefit to Source to create entities that assist those in the physical to create and be. Because they can help a physically manifested being find resonance with what it wants and its original purpose- and perhaps, more importantly, because they help- the physical become aware of and therefore resonate with Source.

To become aware of your higher self and resonate with Source is to truly thrive in your physical existence. More evolution comes in the universe of a thriving physical existence than ever came of a suffering physical existence. We become an energetic vibrational match to guides who are masters in the lessons, abilities, and problems that we are engaged in. They aid our growth. They never see us in the light of success or failure. They have a completely objective view. Just like Source, they are only of service to our highest good. These entities gain and learn from the experience of this being as well. Their evolution is best served by a format that is not expressed in the physical, which is why they chose to project into thought form but not physical form. They may choose to convey a name to you, because it is easier for a person who is experiencing a physical existence and point of view to relate to a singular being than a thought form that is not singular. They know the truth of non-separation, so some will not give a name because it is their wish to convey the truth of oneness. They are everywhere, they are wonderful, and you can learn to find energetic vibrational resonance with them and experience them with your senses as well if it is your desire to do so. They can almost always perceive us better than we perceive them. To them, there is no time and no space as we perceive time and space to be. They are often able to manipulate electric currents.

Developing intuition is very important if it is your desire to experience them as an entity. Most often, their messages are felt as our own knowledge, our own thinking, or an unexplainable sensation. To be able to experience them, one must learn to alter their own energetic vibration to find resonance with their very high vibration, which is a vibration that is usually out of range of our own. Guides may choose to portray a personality and life story that you relate to. Often this takes the form of a projection in the form of an image of themselves from a past life you both lived in the physical together. It is just a point of relation or resonance with you in this life.

Angels are also a type of guide. Often they are the least manifested, and therefore the most vibrationally resonated with Source itself. Though they do not often project themselves with the image of wings, the traditional image of a person with wings is an image they have chosen that has helped people identify what they are and what their purpose is. They use the imagery of wings because wings have long been a symbol of a spiritual messenger when Judeo-Christianity came about. It was a symbolic image that resonated very strongly with the people who were alive at that time. Because of the overwhelming Christian influence that still exists today, this is a symbolic image that speaks to people of their purpose. They can and do still show up in this way if it is the format that will best be received by whomever they are relating with. They very much want you to know that they have information for you from Source itself. When they lower their resonance to the level of physical understanding, they will communicate with a person in a wide variety of ways.

One cannot address the idea of interdimensional communication without approaching the subject of intuition and psychic abilities. Psychic ability is basically the ability to perceive information hidden from the five immediately obvious, three-dimensional, physical senses which are sight, taste, sound, touch, and smell. For some, the very word "psychic" is charged with negative associations. As it usually happens with enigmatic concepts that suggest there is more than what immediately meets the eye, it has become a term that some have lumped in with pseudoscience and self-delusion. It is an unfortunate reaction that cuts people off from their true nature, because everything that is in existence is an interpretation of what is ultimately an energetic vibration. There is much more information being received and broadcast than what is physically visible or logic-based.

We are all interpreting energy to be able to even form a three-dimensional reality out of that energy. Therefore, it is within everyone's capability to be psychic. In fact, everyone is psychic but most people just either don't have conscious awareness of it or are so accustomed to it that they attribute their insights to common sense when it would not actually be common sense for anyone else. You would be hard-pressed to actually find someone who has never had an extrasensory experience. The problem starts when a person is exposed to an experience that is undeniable but seems to fit outside the box of understanding that makes up their current reality. The universe has provided that person with a gift of an opportunity for expansion and ascension past their current understanding. However, people tend to be fear based, and getting outside the box of our own understanding seems very uncomfortable to us.

The choice is to either proceed into the unknown or to limit oneself to what already is. Often a person will then take this undeniable experience and attempt at all costs to rationalize it and cram it into the box of his or her current reality- one that fits this person's definition of what is possible and what is not. Logical reasoning muffles the internal voice of intuition that is always there, whether we listen to it or not. That which is nonphysical or spiritual in nature is always operating, whether a person believes in it or not. An intuition is an internal knowledge without any conscious awareness of how you have that knowledge. Instincts are an example of intuition, which are as natural as our other physical senses and as natural as emotion.

To be able to consciously access and interpret information in energy that is non-manifestational in nature at will is different. This is when intuition- which is natural- becomes a cultured skill you can use to your benefit as well as to the benefit of all that is. It can become quite difficult and can require great skill to operate on a level of awareness of energy that is not physical in nature or in accordance with oneness to decipher what source the energy is coming from as well as to separate the energy of one thing from the energy of another. The accuracy of psychic impression relies heavily on the ability to achieve an unbiased state. But with conscious attention, intuition can get to the point that one can search for and subsequently tune in to specific energetic vibrations exactly like someone would tune to a channel on a radio station.

There are many people who can consciously read energy that exists beyond the third (tangible) dimension. Energetic imprints are often left in places where a high-energy event took place. People can tune into that event, even when a large measure of time has passed since the event occurred. People can read energy on objects, interpret energy fields around physical things visually, hear things that are not within physical hearing range, and pick up information telepathically and empathically. They can channel energy that is not manifested in the physical by first tuning into it and then allowing themselves to act as an objective interpreter for that energy so it can express itself in the physical through that person.

It is even possible for some to read the future, because everything in the future is an exact energetic match to what a person is thinking in the present. The thoughts that you are thinking right now cook up the cocktail that will be your future. A future reading is not the foretelling of a future that is set in stone, but it is in fact nothing more than a deciphering of probabilities. If a person's thoughts change, then his or her future will change too. What gives some clairvoyants tremendous accuracy in predicting the future is that people are very often habitual creatures and do not change their thought patterns, even though they have the opportunity to do so at any point in their lives.

A premonition is a kind of insight into what you are creating right now with your current thoughts. Indeed, the probable outcome is that an energetic vibrational match to what the thoughts of society- or even the human race- is thinking will often be received as a premonition through dreams. Dreaming is a mode in which the brain is in a state of non-judgment and is therefore much more able to receive vibrational information that goes beyond the physical. Energy is constantly being absorbed and transmitted through our nervous system. The energetic vibrations in and around us are constantly being processed in us through thoughts, emotions, and even our physical bodies.

Psychic information comes to different people in different forms that people often do not recognize. For example, they can come to someone in the form of emotionally charged impressions, such as an intense feeling of fear, bliss, or grief that seems to come from nowhere. They can come in the form of physical sensations like being short of breath, sweating, or pain in certain areas of the body that are unexplainable. They can come in the form of images, visions, voices, or dreams.

No matter how intuition surfaces, everyone can learn to develop conscious use of it. There are many techniques that people have come up with over the last century for developing psychic reception. Learning to decipher psychic information is no different from learning a different language. You may be overwhelmed and discouraged at first, but in time, you will recognize patterns within this language and derive meaning out of what feels like chaos. If you make it your intention and desire to recognize intuitive impressions when they come up and develop this natural ability into a skill, you will begin to notice psychic impressions when they do surface, and you will be drawn to the exact circumstances that are conducive to your psychic development. We are always on a path to greater understanding and discovery. The greater understanding you have about your intuition, the greater your knowing of Source will be, and the greater control you will have in your life.

CHAPTER 6
YOUR PHYSICAL HEALTH:
YOUR PHYSICAL LIFE

The flesh is fleeting
a moment in time
the gift of lip and fingertip and prime
born of the cognition of each being
a body,
a manifestation of divine.

There are many levels on which a person could address the subject of physical health. Everything about this physical life that you lead is experienced through your body. When your body is in a state of health, it reflects all aspects of your mind. What is overlooked in society today is that the reverse is even truer. When your mind is in a state of health and therefore connected to its spiritual origin, it reflects itself in all aspects of your body. The reason that spirituality is such an essential ingredient to the health of your physical self is that the entire reason for your physical existence is one of spirit, or Source. When you lose touch with that purpose of spirit, you lose touch with the purpose and role of your thoughts. When you lose touch with the purpose and role of your thoughts, you lose touch with the purpose and role of your emotions. When you lose touch with the purpose and role of your emotions, you stop thinking that how you feel is of paramount importance in your life. Once you lose touch with the fact that how you feel should be of paramount importance in your life, you are becoming okay with maintaining an energetic vibration that will ultimately lead to physical ailment.

On the level of our physical body, the study of healing is a scientific and artistic one. It uses external things such as medicine, physical therapy, surgery, herbs, massage, aroma, sound, nutrition, sleep, and exercise to influence the body to come back into alignment with health. Each of

41

these techniques can be incredibly useful if a body has manifested illness. It is incredibly difficult to find a good-feeling thought if you feel terrible physically. Body medicine can be a sort of knight in white armor if used as a tool to correct or abate a problem once it has fully manifested just long enough for someone to find a stable platform from which to change the way they think and realign with their higher self. Sometimes a physical tool is all it takes for a person to mentally release their extraordinary resistance to the energetic vibration of health and believe their way to wellness.

The medicines, surgeries, and physical therapies that exist today would not exist if they did not serve a profound purpose. Sometimes, despite good intentions, this purpose causes so much negativity that the entire practice of body medicine must evolve. Sometimes its purpose is to force someone to a point where they must start looking outside the traditional box of physical science and body medicine and reconnect with other modalities of healing. Sometimes its purpose is to truly aid our journey through the physical in a joyful and productive way.

Everything in existence today has its own energetic vibration. It is ultimately a choice whether we pick up those vibrations and make them our own. As we explore our physical dimension, it is quite easy to be influenced enough to find resonance with things we are around. While this can serve to greatly increase our disease, it can also be used to our advantage. In spending time around a thing, ingesting it, listening to it, or smelling it, it is possible to assume its energetic vibration. Certain energetic vibrations cannot find resonance with the energetic vibration of specific ailments and therefore upon assuming the energetic vibration of that thing, the ailment must not manifest.

A good example of this is the example of aspirin. Aspirin is acetylsalicylic acid, which is the main component of willow bark. Acetylsalicylic acid has an energetic vibration that cannot find resonance with the energetic vibration of thromboxane, which binds platelet molecules together within blood vessels and helps people prevent the manifestation of blood clots. A person could receive the same effect by using an extract of willow bark, smelling willow bark, hearing music played on an instrument made of willow. Or spending time near and focusing on the bark of willow trees. All that prevents a person from receiving this same effect by using these different techniques is getting stuck in the modality of physical science of the body. The person believes in the fact that aspirin will work and does not believe the others will work, and so the others will not. If the person harbored a strong belief that the aspirin would not work, it also would not.

The body manages to simultaneously be a very simple and complex system that allows us interaction with this physical dimension. Nowhere is this dichotomy more obvious than in DNA. In essence, DNA is the very first manifestation of a blueprint of Source's idea of you. It is the meeting place of the spirit and the physical. For years, we have been stuck in three-dimensional awareness and have therefore seen DNA as purely three-dimensional in nature. This is not only inaccurate, but this also stops us from being able to see the whole picture of our reality, purpose, and eternal nature. DNA, like everything else, has a magnetic field, and as such, it is not restricted to the third dimension. It is interdimensional. It is both physical and nonphysical. In fact, more of our DNA is nonphysical than physical in nature. The part that we physically see as biological and hereditary matter is dwarfed by the amount of nonphysical energy going into that DNA which is informational in nature.

Many people think that they are restricted to living out what is encoded in their DNA as if it were a life sentence. It is the scapegoat of many problems, from obesity to deformity. DNA is really like a group of cards that have been all picked out and assembled by Source as the concept of you, so it is now your choice how to play those cards. You can increase or decrease the ways the DNA communicates with the molecules and cells in your body. DNA is not determining your thoughts, way of life, or physical health. It is an idea that manifests physically and is constantly being amended by your thoughts and re-informing your body how to be. It is only a control tower of thoughts being broadcast to your body. The thoughts, however, control DNA.

This is where the modality of thought, or mind medicine, trumps all that could possibly exist as a modality of healing in the realm of body medicine. It is in this respect that people suffering from ailments and doctors of body medicine hold extraordinary power. We are used to seeing the world in an external context, so we tend to trust the advice of people outside of us who we believe know better than we do and have devoted time to the study of one thing or another. In trusting their advice and knowledge, we believe the thoughts they lend to us. And believing is being. Therefore, when a doctor looks at the odds, which lend to their belief, and conveys them along with the belief to a patient, the patient will most likely assume that belief and make it their own. If there is one thing that a doctor should do above all other things to help people suffering from any ailment, it should be to convince these people of their own ability to heal. There is no such thing as something in the physical that is static. No matter what the statistics and odds tell you, anything that has manifested in the physical in the first place has the ability to change. Though any ailment is potentially terminal, there is no such thing as an ailment that is terminal in and of itself. Nothing exists in this physical world that, with or without changes being made, has a decided outcome.

Mind, or thought, is the bridge between spirit and body. You find harmony in your spirit with your thoughts, and you use thoughts to create harmony in your body. Your entire body originated as a thought. When your thoughts change to match an energetic vibration that is negative, it is as good as rewriting the blueprint of your body- so this negative change must manifest as illness. Every illness on the planet today is the result of adopting negative thought patterns and resonating with negative energetic vibrations. Chronic disease is in fact caused by chronic thoughts such as those of fear, stress, guilt, resentment, hate, and of the feeling of being overwhelmed. If there is no weakness present in the pre-manifested vibrations of thought, there is nowhere for illness or traumatic injury to occur, so there is no way for a virus or bacteria to effect you, and your genetic predispositions toward a particular disease will be dormant.

At first glance, you may find yourself balking at this concept. After all, we are taught that the world exists outside of us. We are taught that we have no control over things outside of ourselves. You have probably grown up thinking that if you were to travel at eighty miles an hour down the freeway and someone were to lose control and crash into you, there would be no way to avoid it. It would not be your fault, and you could not prevent the injuries that result as just a matter of odds and physics. According to the way we were taught, if a virus existing outside of you is seeking a host cell and finds one, you will get sick, whether you want to or not.

We have been practicing this pattern of thought for so long and the Law of Attraction has been yielding those results to us for so long that it is easy to understand why it would scarcely be conceivable for us to think any other way. But what you are doing in that moment is pointing at the physical proof of your life and saying that proof is the reason you feel the way you feel. The truth is that the only reason the proof even exists in the first place is because you feel the way you feel. You cannot experience the car accident in the first place if you were not practicing thoughts that made you, previous to the event, an energetic vibrational match to a car accident. If you were not practicing thoughts that made your body open to weakness, you could not experience injury as a result of that car accident or be the victim of a virus or bacteria of any kind. In fact, it is our very belief that we can be affected by anything outside of us that makes it so.

A person could potentially live their entire life without ever getting to the point that illness or pain physically manifests in their experience. However, at this phase in our evolution, most everyone has or will experience these things at some point in their lives. It is for this reason that every modality of healing has value. One of the best ways to address a problem that has manifested is to address it on all levels of body, mind, and spirit. You are more than a body. Your body is a reflection of your mind, and both are functions of the spirit, or Source. The reason that the mind is the most essential aspect of healing is that no matter how much you do on the physical level to change circumstances that have already manifested, they will continue to manifest again and again if the thoughts you are habitually thinking remain the same.

It is very easy to fall into the path of shortsightedness and say that an illness comes from a specific virus and that you know this because you can see it hacking into cells with a microscope. This is the same as telling the story that the light which illuminates a room comes from a light bulb. The story of where light itself actually comes from can be traced much further than that. It is a much longer story, just as the story of an illness is much longer than what is obvious and visible, which we often call the cause. When you trace illness back farther than the thing you call the obvious cause, you will find that negative thought, which is what prevents connection to the energy the Source part of you is focusing through you at all times, is the root of all illness. Just like you cannot eliminate a weed when all you continue to address is what is above the ground, you cannot eliminate an illness if all you continue to address is what you can see, or what is tangible in the physical dimension.

It is your thoughts that create your reality. While there is nothing wrong with identifying a problem first so as to better figure out what to focus on by way of a solution, it is very logical that once an illness has occurred, it would grab your attention and you would become oriented in the direction of the problem rather than the solution. You would start to notice how you feel, focus on what is wrong with you, and worry. And so you would have thoughts of the worst-case scenario. You would then start talking about the problem with family and friends, and then you would go to a doctor's office where the entire purpose of the visit is to search for something that is wrong. In all of this, you will have given the energetic vibration of illness, pain, and "wrong with me" so much focus that you would amplify it and it would continue to get worse and worse.

If you are able to find a way to distract your mind from focusing on the ailment you are suffering from at any given time and find a feeling of relief in thoughts that are truly positive about your life, improvement of that ailment will occur. Also, if you find a way to focus as strongly and solely on what it would look and feel like to be in perfect health—as you most often focus on the ailment— the ailment would improve so rapidly that you will beat any odds that had been laid out before you. Any practitioner of any kind of medicine is only as good as you allow them to be. Belief is everything here. If a person believes they will get better, they are right. If a person believes they will not get better they are also right. If it makes you feel secure to go see a medical doctor, then going there is beneficial. If instead it makes you feel afraid and out of control, then going there will prevent healing. If it makes you feel hopeful to go see a holistic or energy healer, then going there is beneficial. If instead it makes you feel skeptical and expect illness to remain, then going there will prevent healing.

We have the power to focus on anything we choose to focus on. The reason that it doesn't feel like we do is that when a thought is practiced often, the neurons in your brain that translate that thought actually form a definitive connection, which form a long-term relationship with each other. You could think of this very definitive connection between specific neurons as a "neuro-rut," because you get stuck in that mode of thinking. The thought that causes a very specific biochemical response in your brain has become so practiced that like anything else done in repetition, it takes no effort to think it, and the biochemical results are immediate. They are so immediate, in fact, that it doesn't feel as though you've initiated the thoughts. Because the Law of Attraction is working on all levels of reality, it also works on your thoughts. This means that when you have a thought, it will attract another thought that finds resonance with the first thought— and before you know it, you have snowballed into a negative spiral of thought that is now making itself manifest in the physical dimension.

It is possible, however, to snowball in the opposite direction with positive thoughts. In time, you can purposefully create a positive neuro-rut in your brain that will feel so effortless you will not even feel as though you initiated it. Most focus in any form of medicine should be given to prevention rather than dealing with an illness once it has manifested. The way to do this is not to focus on potential problems, but rather to focus on health. Once you focus on positive thoughts, which will find resonance with your higher self, you will eventually achieve health.

You will find that not much effort has to be lent to trying to force yourself into a healthy lifestyle of diet, sleep, and exercise. When you attune yourself with positive thoughts, you will be naturally inspired toward things in the physical that are an energetic vibrational match to health, and your impulses will travel in that direction. Any action that is inspired by a bad-feeling place rather than a good place should never be taken, thus any action inspired by a good-feeling place or thought should be taken immediately. You will notice when you start to do this that nothing worth doing is hard to do. Inspiration is your higher self calling you forward toward action, and when your higher self is initiating an action, it is effortless.

In the arena of mind medicine, you will hear much talk of energy work with regards to auras. Auras are essentially part of the "Tulpa" you. They are part of the thought form that all people are. An aura contains information which it emits. It also absorbs information, because it is highly perceptive and sensitive to information in the environment surrounding it. You could think of it like an electromagnetic form of consciousness that both transmits and receives to and from you. Some people with energetic vibrations that are high enough to find resonance with thought forms can interpret them through their senses. All people have the capability of experiencing auras.

They exist around all things. The aura is a more expansive part of you than your physical body. This energy field is constantly lending to, as well as emanating from, your physical body, and to anything you interact with in the physical. Auras can be interpreted as having different sounds, sizes, shapes, patterns, textures, and colors. They vary greatly in color in terms of hue and value. The aura colors are perceived because the distribution of light particles versus the wavelength in an energetic field varies greatly and is therefore perceived differently by the human eye.

Any or all of these characteristics of an aura can tell a practitioner of energy work what areas need to be focused back into a beneficial resonance. Auras can tell a nearly complete story of who you are. Your aura will respond to the thoughts you are thinking and change its characteristics to match that thought. If you are thinking a negative thought with enough regularity, it will show up in this thought form first, and then it will show up in your physical body. You could think of your aura as the visible blueprint mirroring the thoughts you are thinking and the thoughts that lead to your identity in this moment. This includes attitudes, memories, beliefs, experiences, and more. It includes basically anything this life as well as past lives has caused you to become. Your aura is the blueprint for the building of the physical you.

As a secondary therapy to changing the thoughts that the problem originates from, which are the "thoughts of the architect making the blueprint," you can focus on your aura, or "blueprint," in order to teach it a different and healthy energetic vibration. There is no such thing as a person who is able to heal someone else. It is always a choice for someone to adopt or not adopt an energetic resonance in line with healing. Healers are, for lack of a better word, teachers who offer an energetic vibration to someone that they then have the ability to resonate with or not resonate with. Every person has the ability to teach others to heal themselves with the example of their own energetic vibration. A practitioner of energy work has become very adept at this—not only by using the very high energetic vibration of their own aura to influence another person's aura into resonance with their own, but also by using their own thoughts to influence another person's vibration into resonance with those thoughts. Naturally, the energy field has many natural channels of energy flowing in both ingoing and outgoing patterns, which helps maintain your physical form and life. These have traditionally been called meridians and chakras.

In the center of the palm, there is a point that the Chinese healers have long called the "Laogong point." This point is located where there is a very prominent outputting energy channel. A person can use their own hands on their own body, or on others to infuse energy that is naturally being emitted from this point in their hands. This technique of energy healing with the hands—which is the most traditional and widely used technique—can be used to help a person find a positive resonance, no matter what ailment they suffer from. You do this subconsciously when your physical body gets injured and your immediate reaction is to hold the injured part of your body in your hands.

When you or someone you see is suffering from an ailment, one of the best ways to help yourself or help someone find healing is to hold an image of you or that person thriving and in perfect health in your mind. See the part of yourself or them that is discordant as being back in resonance. If, for example, someone has a cold, focus on the image of their sinuses completely clear, picture their voice sounding perfectly normal, and picture them excited and full of energy. Picture this person saying, "I feel totally better now." If this is difficult to do, you can use an image like that of light or a specific color permeating the affected area of their body and healing it. The images you could use are limitless. When you have picked one that is a correct energetic match to healing, you will know, because the image will make you feel good. Even with regards to other people, when you are doing something that is right for them, it will register in your experience as positive emotion.

People intuitively know what is in line with health and what is not. It is for this reason that you do not need to look outside yourself for this, or ultimately any answer.

CHAPTER 7
WHERE THE SCULPTING
OF YOUR LIFE
GOES WRONG WITH WORTH

Without all ornament yet with substance
still, potential still remains.
To value oneself is no kind of false art form.
Is worth so faint a thing to perceive?
The seasons of life that cover it in complex
cobwebs would have you forget
That potential is worth
and all that dies around it, leaves it green.

The majority of human suffering on the planet today is the result of the fact that we have forgotten the purpose of our lives. Along with that loss of memory, we have developed a flawed perception of worth and happiness.

Worth is defined as the quality that renders something desirable, useful, or of quality. But the question is, to whom is something desirable, useful, or of quality?

The reason so many people are not living the lives they were born to live is that after a certain amount of time in this physical life, the opinions of others began to matter more than the opinions they have of themselves and the opinions their higher self has of them. It is understandable, because we have lost knowledge of our intention in coming down to this life with other life forms than just ourselves. This intention is to use what we see around us, as well as each other, to gain better clarity about what we want and love and to give birth to new thoughts that the universe will then become.

In the beginning, we did not see the opinions others held about the world to be a threat to us. But once we made other people's opinions our own and began the quest to make others conform to us in order to feel validated, we did see them as a threat. Now, as people, we are in the perpetual cycle of trying to please those outside us, which is an impossible task. In trying to please those outside us, we started to define our worth and quality by how desirable and useful we were to others. We began to feel the need to struggle toward approval in order to justify our own existence. In that moment, we decided we had to prove ourselves to be worthy of worth.

The flaw in this is thinking you have something to prove. Your reason for existence goes far beyond what you do in this life and even who you are in this life. Your existence in the physical dimension is all the justification you will ever need of worth. To Source, your worth has never been in question. Your intention in coming into the physical dimension was never to measure your value against others or to come to the conclusion that anything or anyone is better than you. Your intention in measuring yourself against others was to use that observation as a means to know what you want and become that. We do not all want the same things, and so when you try to become something that someone else tells you that you should want to be, you are defeating your entire purpose of being here. "Should" is an empty motivation giving rise to one of the most painful emotions of all—guilt. In following the motivation of another person thinking you "should," you are putting a wall between the connection between you and your higher self. In doing so, you will live a life full of suffering, just as the people who are looking at you in this moment and saying that you need to be something that is in line with their own desires instead of your own are living lives full of suffering. The only thing you should measure yourself against is your own bliss.

No life is a failure. Every life, no matter how much suffering is a part of it, is giving birth to the evolution of Source. Some people will not realize the evolved version of reality, which is bliss, until they die. But you have the power at any moment to fully realize your own bliss. To do this, you have to stop living life according to accomplishment, other people's ideas of importance, and the desires of others. Start living life according to your own desires and your own ideas of importance. Make bliss your life's purpose.

If you do this, you will have achieved the energetic vibration of your higher self. You will be living as your highest self in the flesh. All the things you have ever wanted, which is what your higher self has become because of your wanting, will come to be with little to no effort on your behalf. If you go against your own bliss, you will find that everything you are trying to force yourself to become, do, and force into existence takes a great deal of effort. When you try to do those things, you will become exhausted and potentially fail at them, at which point you will then say, "I am worthless." If you put bliss before all else on your priority list, you will enjoy everything you do. You will enjoy it because the emotion of enjoyment happens when you have the pure energy of Source with you in those thoughts you are thinking and actions you are taking and thus, they will feel effortless. In that effortlessness and success you will say, "I am worthy." It is only from this living of your own happiness that you can ever come to feel worthy, help people become happy, or be of value to anyone outside yourself. To say your bliss should be your life's goal is an understatement. What should be said is that bliss should be the goal you have at all moments of every day of your life.

The idea of evolving and changing is something that we often resist as humans, because if we have issues with self-worth to begin with as most of us do, we extract a hidden meaning from the idea of change. We extract the hidden meaning that we are not good enough already. If we are not good enough exactly as we are, then we can't be loved exactly as we are, so we are not loveable, and therefore, not loved. This couldn't be further from the truth. Our worth has nothing to do with *who* we are in personality traits, our physicality, or our behaviors in any moment, because that is always temporary. If your worth was caught up in the traits that come along with being human, your worth would be lost to you once you were dead. This is not the case. At the same time, worth has everything to do with what you are, because what you are in every moment is potential energy.

This brings us to the concept of acceptance. As is the case with syntax, the word acceptance carries with it different meanings for different people. Some of these meanings are beneficial, while others are detrimental. On the positive end of this word is the concept of making peace with what is. When you are fighting against something by not accepting it, you are introducing friction into your life by trying to push against something you cannot rid your life of. Any attention to it reinforces it instead of eradicating it. To accept in this way is to let go of resistance, thereby allowing your focus to attend only to what you do want in your life experience. You cannot experience positive change if you do not let go in this exceptionally expansive and loving way. To accept healthily is to understand what is and adopt it only as what is—not with the frustration that it is. You are living nothing but the manifestation of your previous energetic vibrations of which you cannot change because they are only things that have been. Frustration at what has been binds you to what has been. Healthy acceptance sets you free.

On the unhealthy end of acceptance, you have resignation to what is. Whether you like it or not, negative acceptance means consenting to what is in order to force yourself to approve of it, to consider it right, or worse, to consider it permanently true. To consider something permanently true is to make it static, or to condemn yourself to vibrationally repeat what is. It is also to miss the impermanent nature of this universe. Acceptance, as it should be used, does not mean settling for, tolerating, enabling, or validating. It simply means to practice unconditional love by releasing yourself from negative focus and discontinuing the combat against anything, which only keeps it in your life.

It is of paramount importance to accept where you are and who you are. It is also of paramount importance to accept where and who others are. Though it always feels very good to be accepted by others, it is not the key to happiness. This is why having a desire for acceptance from others means you are experiencing a lack of acceptance not because of them, but because of yourself. When you do not vibrationally emit acceptance of yourself or others, you cannot be an energetic vibrational match to people who accept you. A key ingredient to happiness is healthy acceptance of yourself and others. If you have acceptance for yourself and others, you will not desire acceptance from anyone, and so you will not need it. It will be abundant in your life. Healthy acceptance allows you to let go of resistance to what is and pave a clear road for positive change. To look at a behavior, personality trait, or physical thing that you dislike in yourself and say, "Well, this is who I am so I must force myself to like it" or to tell someone else to do the same thing because they must love it to love you is going against the way this universe is intended to work.

All people are intended to look for things and create things they like, not force themselves to try to like things they don't like. This is a losing battle. It is also to try to make that temporary trait you are confusing with worth on principal a permanent part of you. This makes no sense when it is often the energetic vibration of that trait or way of thinking that is in question, which is causing you to feel negatively and attract what you don't want into your life. It's not about changing yourself because you feel you are unlovable if you don't. You are loved in every moment by Source. You can learn to love yourself again at any moment. Love has nothing to do with what you're intending to change.

The better people get at creating their own lives, the better they will be at the kind of loving that is not conditioned upon any externals. Indeed, it does not have to include externals unless they choose to focus on some of the externals they do like about you to further appreciate you. It only holds you back from bliss when you are not okay with change because you're confusing negative acceptance with real love. It only holds you back when you demand others to like all of you as well as all of your detrimental energetic vibrations because you don't like them. If you did, they wouldn't be causing you to feel negative emotions, and it wouldn't matter to you what they thought. Needing acceptance from others holds you prisoner with bars between you and bliss. Not accepting yourself or others also holds you prisoner with bars between you and bliss. To accept is to take your power back. You no longer need something outside to change in order to practice unconditional love.

Acceptance is the key to unconditional love. The reason you cannot be loved if you don't first love yourself is that you cannot hold the energetic vibration of self-distaste and hope to attract anything other than what matches exactly with that energetic vibration. If you could get love without giving love, there would be no evolution in this universe. Nothing would have a reason to change, and everything would stay exactly as it is. Being able to get love without first finding out how to love goes against the laws of the universe for very good reason. Fall in love with what you do love about yourself or someone else instead of trying to force yourself to love what you don't like about yourself or someone else. Fall in love with what you do love about yourself rather than demanding that others love what you don't like about yourself in order for you to feel loved. Use what you don't like about yourself or others to inspire you to find out what you would like instead. Focus on the knowledge that your real worth lies in the fact that you are Source energy, and as such, you can become whatever it is that you would like to be instead.

You do not need to be perfect. To stand in perfection is impossible, because this life is an ongoing process of evolution. The perfection is in the process instead of in the end result. When a baby is born, we do not look at it and say that it does not have worth because it is not perfect yet.

There is no point at which there is a line drawn in the sand after which a person should be completed or perfect. A portion of our problem with ourselves and others is that we like to draw that imaginary line at a certain point in a person's journey into adulthood and expect perfection from ourselves and others from that point on. When we realize we have not been living in resonance with our idea of perfection, we tend to doubt and judge ourselves instead of realizing that perfection is not a decided point that we must live up to. Perfection changes as we think it into being. When a child is born, we do not expect the child to be perfect, because we do not expect the child to know what we know. However, we often expect ourselves to know everything, and we expect others to know everything we know.

There are two points of view at all moments—spiritual knowledge and physical life knowledge. Source's point of view and knowledge are unanimous—it is in everyone, it is eternal, and it always agrees. The life perspective point of view and knowledge is completely dependent upon what the individual has observed and their own life experience. This is where it becomes a stance of condescension and war. If we begin assuming that everyone has had the same life experience we have, we start assuming they should have the same point of view and therefore agree with us. When they don't, it causes us to doubt ourselves or defend ourselves and become angry at them over the pain we experience due to that energetic discord.

There is a large chasm between where they are and where you think they should be, and between what they think and what you think they should think. This is because from your point of view and life experience, you are implying that what is best for them is what you have decided is best for you due to your life experience. Assumption about what is right or wrong has only to do with one thing, and that is life experience—but life experience is different for every single living thing. The idea of right and wrong varies from person to person. It is entirely based on beliefs. What is true from the physical point of view is just observation of what has manifested due to previous energetic vibrations being focused into being. Physical truth is in the eye of the beholder. This is why we will never come to a decision about what is right or wrong for all living things. It is a very individual thing between a person and their higher self.

When a person is going against their higher self, which is what we call "wrong," they will feel the negative discord associated with that lack of energetic resonance. When a person is in agreement with their higher self, which is what we call "right," they will feel the positive resonance of that energetic entrainment. In order to understand what is right for another person as well as what is true, you would have to be looking at that person, and life itself, from the eyes of their higher self. We cannot do that from the point of view of our separated physical life experience. In forcing someone into a way of being or thinking, you are forcing them against their own right. A person must come to that on their own—and that is a process. If someone has a belief that disagrees with the view of their higher self, such as the belief that it is right to participate in genocide, it does not matter what action you take from your point of view, or the view that genocide is wrong and peace is right. Any action you take from that vantage point will be a tiny shadow of the discord being experienced by the person participating in genocide due to their disconnection with their higher self in that choice.

The Law of Attraction brings those who resonate with punishment and murder the exactness of that resonance. If you could just trust that every person has the ultimate teacher within them at all moments of the day, you would know that the Law of Attraction teaches everyone by being an exact mirror. It is the ultimate justice and the ultimate teacher. It is a reflection that gets larger and larger every time we continue to give it the image, so if it is a positive image, we love it getting larger. If it is a negative image, eventually the reflection gets so big we stand in awareness of it and have no choice but to change—even if change means death. The universe will not let those who stand in opposition of their true selves do it for long. It continues to pull a person forward instead. What may have felt like a closer resonance to your higher self at one time may start to feel farther from resonance with your higher self once you get there. A person may feel better in the resonance of revenge than they did in one of fear, but soon revenge will be the note that is discordant with their higher self. In order to follow the next step of finding resonance, a person may have to move into forgiveness.

One of the best things you can do for yourself is to release yourself from the pressure of being in this state of perfection, release others from having to be in a state of perfection, and trust that you are being pulled forward and they are being pulled forward. If you disagree with each other, you will keep getting the essence of what the other is thinking, and the reflection of that essence when fully realized may serve to change your mind, the other person's mind, or eventually, both of your minds. Everyone will eventually be brought to Source's truth by individual paths. You will not find your bliss in the act of others agreeing with you. This only feels good because at our true core, we all crave the oneness that already is the ultimate truth.

You will not find resonance with your happiness by another person finding resonance with your idea of right. You will find happiness by you finding resonance with your idea of right. If you find resonance with your idea of right, the other person's opinion—however harmful you think it could be—cannot enter your experience unless you wage war with it, which is to find resonance with it. Do not expect yourself to know everything. Do not expect others who are coming from different life experiences to know what you know. Realize that what is right for you is right for you, and that is how it was intended to be. If it ceases to be right for you, which it very well may in this mutable universe, you will know it because it will start to feel wrong for you. If it feels wrong for you and you go in that direction anyway, it will feel more wrong. It will feel more and more wrong until you decide to go in the direction of what feels right, so there is no way to get it wrong. There is no way for anyone else to get it wrong, either.

A part of a person's physical experience and knowledge comes from observing other people's experiences and ideas. The experiences and ideas of another serve us by letting us know what we don't want, or what is wrong for us, and what we do want, or what is right for us. That is the main purpose the experiences and ideas of others were intended to serve in our life. They help us to create, which is the purpose of the book you are reading right now. If we as humans were to stand in total agreement on everything, there would be no evolution, which is the inevitable point of physical life. Evolution is the inevitable product of going in the direction of your own individual happiness.

CHAPTER 8
WHERE THE SCULPTING
OF YOUR LIFE
GOES WRONG WITH
HAPPINESS

Joy is staring us down, unblinking at every moment.
It is in the golden valleys of a ceaseless sky.
It is in the naked and vulnerable nature of a smile
passed from one set of lips to another.
It is in the leisurely taste of an ice cream cone in the summer.
You could wander each and every continent all of your life,
as many often do,
searching for this state called happiness-
and miss the truth in its entirety that you had it all along.
Tangled but ever-present in the spaces between
what you were focused on.
Waiting for your notice.

Our main skewed perception of happiness is that it is dependent on what is outside of you in the people, places, and things in your external environment. But happiness does not have to be dependent on anything or anyone outside of you. *Real* happiness is never dependent on anything outside of you. The minute you start practicing the thought that your happiness depends on other people, how they act around you, and how they feel about you- you have completely given your power away. Indeed, you may have just given up the only power you have in this life, or any life. This physical dimension was set up to be the fairest playing field there possibly could be. Everything you think and feel in the physical dimension is coming to be around you.

Due to the Law of Attraction, anything you ever come into contact with will be the identical replica of what you were thinking and feeling. It was created in this way so it would be obvious and easy to discern whether you liked that choice or wanted to let that inspire you in wanting something better. This physical dimension could really be described as nothing more than an exalted version of everyone getting a dose of their own medicine. You can't ever have a taste of anything in the universe that is not a taste of your own medicine—both the best and the worst of it. To give your power away by saying your lack of happiness is being caused by that which is external to you is to scream at the reflection in the mirror that it is definitely the mirror's fault that you look the way you look.

There is not a criticism in the universe that isn't hypocritical. That doesn't mean that what is hypocritical is that the person's behavior is a carbon copy of the very behavior they are criticizing. It means it is hypocritical in that if you were not offering an energetic vibration that was a match to the behavior you dislike so much, you could not experience the behavior and may not have even experienced the person in their entirety. No problem you ever have is with any other person besides yourself. Every issue is about you. A good example of this is that if a person does not understand that their happiness is not determined by people in their external, they may go to great lengths to try very hard to avoid people who are chronically upset. But in avoidance, a person is identifying what they do not want instead of what they want, and because there is no "anti-note" within the universe (as was talked about in chapter 3), they will continue to hold an energetic resonance with people who are chronically upset. Therefore, chronically upset people will continue to crop up over and over, so much so that the person might feel as though they are being picked on by continually meeting the same people, just different faces.

At the same time, the person who is chronically upset may also have no idea that their happiness is not dependent on external circumstances, so they may try to use other people to constantly help their self out of bad moods. If their happiness is then dependent on these other people to lift their mood, it suddenly becomes threatening that they may come across a fair-weather friend. Because that person is trying to avoid these types of friends, therefore focusing on the problem, fair-weather friends keep coming up for them over and over again. These two people would very likely continue to blame each other. The fair-weather friend would blame the other's emotional upset as the reason for not being able to be happy.

The chronically upset person would blame the other's fair-weather nature as the reason they are unable to be happy—and neither of them would be right. The precursor to both scenarios is that neither person knows they can control their own happiness, no matter what anyone else says or does.

The best step toward happiness is to get into the habit that when anything shows up in your external environment that you do not like (whether it is a situation, person, place, or thing), immediately turn your attention toward recognition of the precursor within you to the external manifestation. It is just a manifestation of something within you, and it wouldn't have been in your experience if it wasn't an energetic match to something within you. So the question is, what is it?

Many people have been practicing the art of guilt and shame for a long time, so it is necessary to tell you that this should not be a step that leads to guilt, shame, or self-condemnation. It is not your fault. Fault implies blame. There is no one to blame, and this energetic vibration within you that is manifesting negativity is also a large culprit in your evolution toward bliss. It does not matter if it was your intention to assume this vibration or if it was something you assumed by default—you have the total power to change it. This does not have to be threatening. Anything that you see in existence right now is only the tangible evidence of this previous energetic vibration you hold. It does not mean anything more important than that you have found something that if focused into a different energetic vibration will not only attract what you want, but also make it so what you don't want can't come into your space. The best news of all is that once you start recognizing the precursor and then thinking thoughts that change the way you feel, and therefore the energetic vibration you hold within you, your environment will become the exact reflection of that improvement. You will then hold the power that was the power you intended to hold and knew you held in the beginning. You will hold the greatest power there is—the power of your bliss being completely independent of others. When you get into a space of knowledge and you trust that you control your own bliss by controlling your own energetic resonance by choosing what to focus on to the point that you are now doing it, you will then be practicing unconditional love. Your love for others will not be conditioned upon anything they do or don't do. Your love for yourself will not be conditioned upon anything you do or don't do.

Occasionally we have an aversion to the idea of happiness because when we are suffering, people who are very happy can come off as upsetting and fake to us. The reason for this is often because we feel jealousy, which is merely the emotion that we feel when we see what we want but don't think we can have it. We can also develop an aversion to happiness when we are acquainted with happy people who are often unwilling to look at anything they feel is negative. In your moment of isolated pain, you have attracted someone who has left you completely alone. But you should know that these people whose happiness is so upsetting to you are not truly happy. They can be of no benefit to you. Happiness that is dependent on external circumstances is not happiness.

Achieving happiness independent of external circumstances, however, is the surest way for circumstances to change to perfectly match the energetic vibration of your happiness. This is done with selective focus. Happy people (who are not really happy) want to avoid anything negative in nature because they are convinced the maintenance of their faux happiness depends on it. In this way, they paint for us a flawed picture of what happiness is. You cannot be happy if you run from pain, because to run from or try to avoid something is to be focused backward, toward the problem. Real happiness is achieved no matter what people you are around and no matter the circumstances you are in by choosing to focus selectively on the aspects of that person or circumstance that you do appreciate (that which evokes positive emotion) as well as on the thought of how you would wish the person or circumstance to be.

Truly happy people see the value in negativity. They no longer fear it, because they see the purpose of it. In a world that sees dirt as a negative, it is like seeing the dirt's worth to the flower. If there is no dirt, there is no flower. The energetic vibration of avoiding negativity is in complete opposition to the energetic vibration of embracing the positive. It is possible to embrace the positive in the negative by embracing the feeling of negativity itself. Many people fear that to embrace negative emotion is to keep it in your life and to get stuck in it when the truth is exactly the opposite. When you learn to embrace negative emotion and you release your extreme resistance to it, you are introducing a contradictory energetic vibration to it that is so strong, it cannot maintain itself. It will dissipate entirely.

That which is negative is natural to this physical dimension. It is the thing that evokes you to create new wants. It is in becoming those wants that the universe evolves. When you embrace negativity and learn to use it for what it is intended, it can no longer hold you captive. You have freed yourself from its previous implications. To be focused positively is also much different than to suppress, devalue, or deny negativity. To do these things is incredibly harmful. The implication of such a mentality is that because the negativity is unresolved, it will keep getting larger and larger—in the same way that it will get larger and larger if all you are focused on is the negative. It also means you are avoiding a perfect opportunity to find more bliss.

If you suppress, devalue, or deny that which is negative, you have lost the extreme value of understanding that can only come from that which we call negativity. You can only seek the opposite of something if you acknowledge the presence of that thing in the first place. By the time you are reading this, you may have practiced a life in which you were out of touch with your own emotional compass for so long it is not immediately obvious what is even causing the negative emotion. If in the moment negative emotion arises you will turn inwards toward it and find where it is coming from, you can expose hidden energetic vibrations within you (the ones that are attracting things like it into your life without you even being aware of it). Once you expose it, you can embrace the feeling with compassion, understanding, love, and appreciation for it. Your negative emotions are like a crying child.

Even anger comes from a vibration of fear. When you embrace the feeling, just like when you embrace a crying child by showing it compassion, the crying stops. Too often, we condemn or fear our negative emotions which are the same as condemning or fearing a small child—the small child that still resides within us. This only makes the problem worse. It is like fighting fire with fire. This awareness you seek out of negativity is not the same as being negatively focused. You are using the negativity to your benefit instead of being stuck in it. Once you embrace that negative emotion, show compassion for it, and gain awareness of it and where it comes from, you can use the one power you have to achieve a positive vibration of focus. In the moment you sit still in your pain or discomfort, face it to understand it, and embrace it to neutralize it, you can then rotate your focus in the direction of what brings about positive emotion.

You can look for positive aspects of anything by focusing on the opposite of whatever you have just exposed. You can take your focus off the unwanted and place it undividedly upon what you would like instead. In this way, instead of getting focused and stuck in negative and thereby attracting more of it to you, you will have used negativity as it was intended to be used—as that which brings you knowledge of what you want to create in your life, your higher self, and this universe. You do not need to seek out negativity since it is an inevitable condition of the physical dimension.

Every new want that you achieve will bring about new comparisons, or problems, to help you further hone the picture of what you truly want. But you do not need to avoid it or feel as though you have failed at deliberately sculpting your life. If your only awareness is of the positive and you see no positivity in that which is negative, you are missing the key point to life in the physical dimension. You are missing an opportunity to find an enhanced state of bliss. If you approach negativity with an attitude of it being an opportunity, you will introduce a vibration that will make it impossible for you to truly suffer at the hands of what is negative. The reason we think that negativity is something to be feared is because people as a whole tend to spend their lives (once negativity crops up) focusing purely on the negative aspects of everything around them in order to justify why they are unhappy. This is because we see our emotion as bad or good instead of the tool that it is. In that judgment, we try to make others and ourselves validate where we are as well as that it is, in fact, not a failure to feel the way we feel because deep down, we feel it is a failure. In truth, it is no kind of failure. You are justified in whatever you feel. You don't have to justify yourself to anyone. You, and you alone, have the power to feel however you want to feel regardless of what is going on in the physical dimension outside of you. The fastest way for you to get to a place of bliss—where you want to be—is to make peace with where you are instead of justifying where you are.

One of the great barriers to being happy is that we have been programmed as people erroneously against our purpose with the idea that going after bliss is selfish, uncaring, and what bad people do. But if you base your life on sacrifice, obligation, and trying to do for others only that which they can do for themselves, you are of no benefit to others. You have taken on the self-imposed role of helping instead of pursuing the bliss one could potentially find in being of value to others. If placing the needs of others above that of ourselves comes from a place of obligation—or worse, if it is the basis of your idea of self-worth—it is a negative energetic vibration and no good can manifest of it. On top of the suffering, it causes you to go against your own bliss on a matter of principle. The people you try to help will resent you for it because the message you are giving them is that you don't think they are capable. You will live your life trying to seek approval and gratitude from others, and you will not receive it. Instead, you will spend your life feeling unappreciated. In turn, you will resent others by seeing them as the reason you feel such a lack of freedom.

It is in trusting others to be able to find their own bliss, enabling them to do so, and not basing our happiness on their decisions that we are of benefit to them. It is only in the maintenance of your own bliss that you will be healthy enough and have enough energy to ever be of benefit to anyone at all. To think that it is selfish to pursue one's bliss is to miss the biggest truth of all—the truth of oneness. If you trace backward, past all the ways that the energy that is Source has manifested into difference, every thing and non-thing in the universe is made of the same exact essence. We are all energy. Even though Source is experiencing itself from the standpoint of separation, it is all a very elaborate virtual reality. We are still just Source expressing itself in different ways. No matter how much it may appear that we are different, we are all one. When you begin to recognize that unity, you will walk throughout the world and see yourself in and as everything that you call other, and you will see everything that is other in and as you.

The state that we traditionally call selfishness is actually a state of deprivation. It is a state in which a person fails to recognize unity and fails to recognize that there is no limit to resources past their own belief that there is. To be selfish is to see others as a threat to your own abundance. This is not the same thing as a person following their own bliss—this is a person working very hard against what doesn't have to be feared in the first place. To be focused on your own bliss is quite different than this. The entire reason that you see this physical dimension from your singular perspective is so you can help Source (yourself) evolve in a much more dynamic way than if we were all to come down and live in a state of consensus. There would be nowhere to evolve if that were the case.

It is this variety and multi-angled point of view that is necessary for Source to know all of itself. It is also a function of the fact that oneness can only be truly known and desired from the standpoint of true divergence. You fulfill this purpose specifically by following your own bliss. Once you realize that you are everything, you will see that in finding your own bliss, you have found it for everything that you call "other" as well. This is, in fact, the very best way to be of benefit to other people, as well as the universe at large, because it is the only strategy over which you have total control. When others experience bliss, you will see it as your own. You will realize that any act of service to another being is also none other than you being of benefit to yourself. In this realization and awareness of the truth of oneness that always was, is, and will always be, you will come to know that there is no such thing as selfishness or unselfishness. When you are everything, everything you do is for yourself. When you are everything, nothing you do is for yourself alone.

There can be another way that sculpting of one's life can go wrong in terms of happiness, and that is when one loses touch with their emotions. After years of practicing thoughts that are not in resonance with our higher self, we often become used to the feeling of that discord. It becomes familiar enough that we don't even register when our emotions are telling us we are off course. We may cut ourselves off from emotions by resisting them to such a degree that we become armored against them and then cannot feel them, even though they exist. We resist them to such a degree that we feel numb. This means that not only are you flying blind through life, but also that you are being controlled entirely by the ego-driven mind instead of by consciousness. We are living entirely from the brain, and the body is not like a living organism—it is like a machine being operated by this brain.

Emotions are the texture of life. When you do not know what it is that your emotions are telling you, it can be very easy to decide erroneously that your emotions are weak and simply write them off as something that makes you feel vulnerable. Often the numbness that is the result is preferable to the idea of feeling hurt. But this pattern of not listening to the intelligence of your emotions leads to great suffering.

It may then be necessary, before embarking on the journey of heeding the advice of your emotional compass, to first get back in touch with your emotions. This may seem like an intimidating task, because in order to train ourselves into this disconnection, we must practice beliefs that emotions are in and of themselves negative and therefore should not be trusted or fought against. First, it is important to realize that even if you are unaware of your emotions, they do exist. They do not abandon you simply because you have not listened to them for quite some time. They cannot abandon you. They are constant. They are like the glue holding the connection between you and Source. Emotions can become accumulated within us when they are repressed. Emotions are always present, even if they are repressed. So all you have to do is find awareness of them again.

If you have awakened to the importance of this reconnection to your emotions, the first step is to acknowledge that this is a true desire of yours, not just a "should." Know that it is the case with every single want you could ever have, that your higher self is drawing that desired thing to you and you to it so you can realize this desire fully. It does not matter if you get back in touch with your emotions with the help of a cognitive therapist or if you are able to re-teach yourself with the exercises to follow. Once this is a desire of yours, whatever way you find to do it is the right way for you.

If you would like to start on your own, you do not need to wait until an opportunity to feel arises (even though this is a good time to become acquainted with emotion) because you can induce feeling for the sake of practice. A good way to induce feeling is with music. Begin by listening to any song chosen at random, and instead of paying attention to the notes, rhythm, or sound, focus your attention inside yourself, looking for the way the song makes you feel. Try this with songs that induce all different kinds of emotions so you can feel the difference in your internal sensations from one song to another. You can dance to the music as well. Dance is a moving expression of emotion.

If you have trouble expressing yourself with words, you may find that expressing your emotion physically is not only a great key to becoming aware of your emotions, but also a way to release tension, thereby making you happier. You can induce emotion by deliberately remembering something as well. Reach for a memory that you think made you feel a certain way. Remember every aspect of this memory. Try to make it as real to you today as it was when it actually happened. The more real it is to you, the more definitive your emotions will be, and the easier it will be to gain a concrete idea of them. Reacquaint yourself with memories that you think made you feel in a wide variety of ways, not just negatively, but positively as well. You can induce feeling in this way with almost everything from movies, to pictures, to fragrances, to foods. The key is to deliberately look to intensify the sensation through your focus. When you stop resisting the experience of the emotion, it will come to you, and with your focus, it will cease to be elusive. Your emotions will become very obvious to you again—like they were when you were young.

When you are in the midst of a current situation in which you don't know how you feel, seize the opportunity. You can begin to do this by finding a place of still observation. Try to observe your internal feelings as objectively as possible. Scan your body, looking for how different parts of your body feel. Suppressed emotion is often canvassed through our physical bodies. Increase your awareness of bodily sensations by taking deliberate notice of any tension, warmth, coldness, tingling, pain, hunger, thirst, or any other physical sensation. It may even come in the form of physical impulse, such as the impulse in your muscle tissues when you desire to hit something. Once you focus on it, the feeling will intensify. Through this process, you will gradually become so familiar with the sensations that you will be able to identify them—even when they are faint and you would not have previously noticed them. Pay special attention to where you feel any sensation.

When you gain awareness of this feeling and can pinpoint it, mentally radiate it out to encompass your entire body. In that conscious intensifying of the sensation, you will make that feeling large enough that you are very aware of it. As you spread it out, feel the sensation becoming not just a function of physical sensation, but of emotional sensation as well. Take objective notice of any thoughts or images that may be coming up. Take objective notice of any memories, sounds, tastes, smells, or physical sensations that may be present within you. You can write or print a list of all the different emotions and have it with you so that you can play a kind of matching game. When you are observing these thoughts, images, physical sensations, or memories, you can circle the emotions you might think they correspond to.

For example, a person may feel very numb during the process of breaking up with a lover, but they have a memory that continues to come up of seeing their parents breaking up years ago. This person could then ask how they felt back then in the midst of that memory and then circle the corresponding emotions on that sheet of paper. From there, the person could then try to deliberately look for the emotions they are currently feeling about the situation at hand and ask if they are the same feelings. The answer is usually a resounding yes, because all thoughts, sensations, memories, images, and other feelings are coming to you because they are a direct mirror of, or match to, your current thoughts. Sit in that emotion and learn it again. Get acquainted with it so it is familiar enough that if it comes up again in the future, you can identify it. You must know what west and north are in order to read a compass, and for this same reason, it is beneficial to label the different feelings once you become familiar with them—feelings such as hopelessness, guilt, or elation—so they become more definite in your awareness and therefore can better guide you.

You may also choose to get in the habit of expressing your emotion when it comes up. You may get to the point that you can identify it. This is very helpful if your habit is to suppress emotion within you. When you feel anger, sadness, fear, or happiness… say so. This intentional affirmation will make the emotion more real, and therefore tangible to you.

CHAPTER 9
THE AXIOM OF IMAGERY

We are one with every single thing we touch and see.
We are part of every rock and beast and tree,
and you are everything you see in me.
In each separate life is present even still-
the truth that we are one and the same
with that which hunts for us
and one with what we kill.
No external thing can be more real
than the one which you in your mind conceal.
For it is none but a reflection of the very same image come to life.
The cadence of the world's terrors shall spring forth from our terrors.
The rhythm of the world's bliss shall spring forth from our bliss.
All the splendor in the world shall be none but the
image of the splendor already present in me.
We are one with every single thing we touch and see.

You are what you touch and see. Upon knowing that, we realize the only truth is one of freedom. It is with that knowledge that you will realize you can change what you touch and see at any moment. In changing it, you will have written the new chapter of the evolution of yourself, this universe, and therefore of Source itself. Every one of us has within us every yet-unrealized potential that exists. Our only limit is our own imagination.

This brings us to the first technique to creating your life the way you want it to be.

When most people think of imagery and visualization, they think of it as purely a visual experience. All sensory perception is the language of imagery. It should be a process that involves sight, sound, smell, taste, touch, and emotion. When you use your mind's eye to see and experience anything the way you want it to be, the energetic vibration of that thought is indistinguishable to the universe as being any different from something that is already in the physical, or that which you call real. Your brain also does not know the difference—and because your brain does not know the difference, your body does not know the difference. The Law of Attraction will bring to you anything that is a match to that energetic vibration—whether that is running the perfect race, getting the perfect mate, or being healthy. Everything in your experience must find resonance with what you are thinking, because it is the law of this universe.

The reason we often get such muddled results is because we have forgotten that the number one power we have in our lives is focus. When we lose touch with focus, just like a muscle that has atrophied from lack of use, the energetic vibration we are sending out to be matched by the Law of Attraction is muddled. We are offering thoughts of success along with thoughts of failure, and we get a mix of both. If the thought we have is one of success we believe we can never have, we never will. Your every experience is a mirror image of your most prominent thoughts, or mental energetic vibrations.

Want is a stepping stone. It can get you in touch with the destination you are headed toward, but if you are stuck in wanting, what you want will never come. You have to think thoughts that make you feel as though you already have what you want for it to completely manifest. This is because wanting is an energetic vibration that resonates with the energetic vibration of not having something, so not having of something is what will continue to manifest. Therefore, it is best to visualize things as if they already are.

You do not have to avoid want as if want itself is the villain. Just see it for what it is and move beyond it into a "having" space. The ways to use this technique are unlimited. Every time you think, you are using this technique of visualization and imagery. The trick is gaining conscious control of it. If you play around with what is available by allowing yourself to be drawn to something when you intuitively feel it may be good for you, you will find what works the best for you. Your aim should be to live something out in your mind as if it was happening now by reaching for the images, sights, smells, tastes, and feelings of it being already. You will know you have chosen the right thought because it will feel good to you.

The better it feels and the more passionate you feel during the exercise, the more intense the energetic vibration you are sending out, the closer to resonance you are with Source, and the sooner it will start to show up in your physical experience.

You can start with an exercise in end-state imagery in which you think of something you want to be true for you. Focus on it as if it is already true for you. Set a timer for ten or fifteen minutes, close your eyes, and live it out completely in your mind. Look for the way it feels, smells, sounds, and looks. Look for reasons it is so fantastic and why you want it. If your thoughts go in a negative direction, without condemning the thought or fighting against the fact that it happened, direct your focus back toward what you want to see. Get as detailed as you possibly can to maintain that good-feeling space you are in while doing it. Continue to do this every day as long as it feels good to do so.

You can also do a simple feeling-state imagery exercise as a way to change from a negative-feeling space to a positive-feeling space. Set the timer again for ten to fifteen minutes and think of images, as if you were going through flash cards, which feel good to you and make you happy. Let each image only come to you briefly by simply trying to see how many you can come up with before the timer goes off. You will end the session in a higher resonance, and you will end up realizing that the world contains much more that is good than is displeasing. The only reason this is difficult to realize in day-to-day life is that most of us are oriented toward focusing on what we don't like. We are oriented toward finding and fighting against the flaw, because we think that is the way to eradicate it—but giving our focus to it only makes it larger.

If you have someone in your life who you are having problems with, set a timer for ten minutes and visualize that person being truly happy, getting everything they truly want, having epiphanies, coming to you for reconciliation, and feeling safe and secure. You will find that in addition to this exercise decreasing your strong feeling of discord toward that person, when you visualize them in true bliss, the negative behaviors you associate with them will also cease to exist, because no one who is truly happy would ever cause suffering to you or to any other life form.

Visualization is a strong tool when you are suffering. You can try a visualization in which you turn to face your pain and visualize it, no matter what type of pain it is, physical or mental. For example, it may look like fire. Once you see what it is, focus on how to cure that image. If your pain did take the image of fire, for example, you could snuff it out with water or dirt. Once the feeling has changed from powerlessness to relief, you can open your eyes.

Another incredibly powerful psychological imaging visualization is one in which you go searching for yourself as a child- your inner child. Take yourself as a child into the arms of you as an adult, introduce yourself, and thank it for being brave. Ask if it has to tell you anything, and explain that its job is done and that it can go to sleep, because you are all grown up. Tell your inner child you can take care of things now and that you love it very much. You can feed it what it would most like to eat, wash it off gently in healing water, and dress it in whatever it most wants to wear. You can help it softly go to sleep in your arms and place it in a warm bed in a very safe, impermeable place you have created for it in your mind. Perhaps you can even put a sleeping pet there with it at the foot of the bed to keep it company and make it feel secure while it sleeps. When you have achieved a good feeling from the exercise, open your eyes and slowly remember where you are in the room.

There are countless resources offering specific guided imagery exercises. Some will resonate with you in whatever space you are in, and others will not. That is okay, because you are the one choosing how to create your experience. Mastery is not the outcome of being in charge of action, but rather, it is the outcome of being in charge of the mind.

CHAPTER 10
THE ANCHOR OF
MEDITATION AND PRAYER

Immortality is ever-present in this playground of birth and death.
Again and again each cycle begins with the
promise that there is more at work here
than living and dying.
This existence which now feels like a
homeland has become your blood,
your sweat, your tears-
its temporary nature forgotten
in the everyday experiences you call your life.
This has become your identity-
it has become your always.
But it is not who you are.
You are the immortal source of all that is.
When you look for it,
you can see it in every face you end up meeting-
you can hear it between the beats your busy heart keeps beating.

When most people think of meditation, the instant image that comes to mind is of a person sitting cross-legged, thumb and forefinger together, with a zoned-out look on their face. Due to a lack of understanding, meditation has taken on the stigma in the western world of being a "hippie" and "hooey" practice that even errs at times on the side of trendiness. Our modern society functions so purely in the physical that meditation has become an impractical practice. This misunderstanding is easily forgivable, because we are a society that degrades the importance of the mind. As such, the true purpose and value of meditation has been lost to us. This is an art form that will come back into daily life for people living in these new times, because meditation is one of the most powerful techniques to apply to the process of sculpting your life.

All meditation is a form of self-inducing a specific state of consciousness. All meditation is designed to help us learn to use our minds instead of continuing the cycle of our minds using us. All meditation is designed to rise to an energetic frequency that is above that of the thinking mind—the mind that is focused purely in the physical dimension. When a person transitions into meditation there is less energetic focus into the physical. The person's brainwaves, which are usually functioning in the form of beta waves, rise in frequency to function in the form of alpha and theta waves. When a brain transitions into this raised frequency, the result is a deep feeling of relaxation. However, relaxation is just a symptom of the real thing that is occurring in meditation. During meditation you are putting yourself into the pure, indiscriminate, receiving mode of Source. This means you are allowing healing, inspiration, and every other aspect that comes along with Source to course through you without introducing any opposing energetic vibration whatsoever.

The word meditation has been used for a plethora of practices. Some of these are practices in which you are setting aside a block of time dedicated to deliberately using your mind, and therefore, they are more like imagery and visualization. Some involve intense training of focus, while others are designed to let go of the mind completely. There is no right or wrong way to meditate. Every meditation (of which there are so many you could not do them all in one life), regardless of the type, has the potential to be incredibly beneficial to you. You will find some of them much harder than others to do. This tells you where you need more practice, but the consistent practice of the meditations you excel in are also integral to your journey.

Meditation is about touching the Source, or spiritual essence that is within all of us. It is about getting into a space where you are removed from the physical as well as your thoughts—enough that you start to become aware that there is a "you" who is watching you. There is a bigger mind that is observing the thoughts you are thinking. In many meditations your breath is used as a focal point, or an anchor of sorts, to your physical body. The reason that using the breath is much more integral to meditation is that your breathing is the easiest way to realize your connection to Source.

Your breathing is much more than just a function of your physical body. When you breathe, the intake of air and release of carbon dioxide is the physical manifestation of what is really happening. When you breathe in, what you are actually experiencing is your higher self filling you up with its focused energy. It is your higher self focusing its energy current into you in order to maintain the creation that is you. It focuses the energy of life into your physical self. This is how you can even stay as an expression in the physical dimension. When you exhale, you are not just releasing discordant energetic vibrations. Your higher self is also pulling from you the energy that your physical self is in this life. Your exhale is an energy current carrying the essence of what this life has caused you to become back to Source so it can evolve from those things. In a simplistic way, you could think of your inhalation, which is the current of your higher self and Source energy into and through you, like electricity sent from a source through a deep sea camera. You could think of exhalation, which is the current of feedback from the physical you to your higher self, like the picture coming back from the camera to the source that sent it down to the bottom of the sea in the first place.

This Source energy is what is keeping you in the physical and alive. You can restrict this current by holding your breath, but to do this is to try to prevent your higher self from forcing itself through you, and you will not be able to do that for long. When you die, your higher self has decided not to focus through you, and this is why you cease to breathe. It is a two-way thing. It is not only that you breathe out to your higher self, but also that your higher self is breathing out to you and breathing you in. The deeper you breathe in life, the more revitalized you will be, because you will be letting in more and more of this Source current. When meditation becomes a practiced, engrained state, your emotions will not have control over your actions as they do now. Instead, you will be consistently seeing the world you live in through the eyes of your highest self, which are also the eyes of Source. From that vantage point, instead of seeing emotions as a force that wrenches you about, you will see them as the trustworthy compass that they are. You will see that the real you is beyond them. The state of transcendence you find in meditation will then be the dominant state in your life. Your negative emotions will not be able to shake the strong footing you now have. It is a kind of freedom you have never experienced. It is the freedom that belongs innately to you.

The further you venture into meditation, the more you can experiment with different meditations and increase the amount of time you meditate. To begin, you can start with the following two meditations:

1) You can start by sitting in clothes that are loose. Sit somewhere that you are most comfortable. It doesn't matter if it is on the floor, in the bed, or on a chair, as long as it is in a quiet location. Set a timer for fifteen minutes. Close your eyes and focus on your breathing. Watch it rise and fall. Just let it come and go in the perfect energy exchange that it is. If a thought comes up, just acknowledge it and let it go, coming back to the breathing. You will find that your mind, at this point (which has not been trained by you into focus), is a bit like a wild horse in that it will continue to run off in tangents of thought. If you get frustrated with the thoughts and the fact that you can't seem to keep your focus solely on the breathing yet, it will only work against you. Instead of getting overwhelmed by the realization of how little control you have over your focus right now, the point is to just observe the thoughts, let them go, and keep directing your focus to your breathing. When the timer goes off, allow yourself some time to reacclimatize to your physical body and physical surroundings. In time, you will find you can focus on your breathing completely for the duration of the time you are meditating. Then, the freedom from thought will clear your mind and put you in the space of complete allowance of Source.

2) You can start by sitting in a comfortable location. Set the timer for fifteen minutes. Start by focusing on your breathing and slowly transition so that for the remainder of the fifteen minutes, you can just be wherever you are. Be completely in the present moment. In the room where you are, observe everything about the present moment without judgment. Notice the sounds you hear, the smells you smell, and the way your clothes feel. Pay attention to your body and the way each part of it feels. If a thought or judgment such as "I don't like that" comes up, just let it go and keep observing. Some people like to do this with their eyes open so they can observe visually as well. Others find this to be distracting from the goal of nonjudgmental observation. Do whatever you feel is easiest. If you

are having trouble with this meditation, you can start to mentally label things without judgment past that. For example, if you hear the hum of the air conditioner, say "air conditioner." If you notice you are holding tension in your shoulders, say "tension." When the timer goes off, come back to focus on the breath, taking at least three very slow, deliberate, deep breaths.

You will find that the more comfortable you become with meditation, the better your life will become. When you are taking time on a daily basis to stop thinking and just be, let go of thoughts that turn you against the magnetic pull of your higher self, and then focus on thoughts that turn you toward the magnetic pull of your higher self, you will start the process of healing. You will start manifesting everything you want to manifest in your life. You will begin the process of living in the state of bliss.

Prayer has held center stage for centuries as the key practice of connecting to Source in nearly every major religion. As such, it has developed a large following of not only believers, but also skeptics. When people have been introduced into an environment that is rampant with beliefs that inhibit the current of Source into physical life, the manifestations that make up that environment are anything but miraculous. The environments created by such beliefs are environments of fear. People try very hard to control the conditions of their fear through external means. It is very easy, then, for people in those conditions to distrust faith. If you are a person who has become convinced due to your life circumstances that your safety depends on controlling what you *can* see, then the idea of believing wholeheartedly in what you don't see (and moreover, that believing *is* seeing) is not only difficult, but also frightening. It is this leap of faith that is the doorway to the universal truth that it is only in the minute you let go that you are ever truly caught.

This decision to let go and to believe before you see is a personal one that no one can be forced into. Sometimes it takes a situation that is so far outside one's control that the person involved has no other available choice. For those who make that leap, prayer can be a catalyst for the change of oneself as well as one's world. It allows the finite to communicate with the infinite. It is the opening up of oneself to becoming a vessel for Source. In doing so, a person can affect the very fabric of reality as we see it. When a person sees the physical evidence of such an effect, they call it a miracle, because it challenges the physical odds and rules that we think are static.

The miracle of prayer has been well recorded throughout history. A person can, upon opening themselves up to Source fully, even direct Source toward another. This is the stuff of spontaneous healing, such as mothers lifting thousand-pound cars off of their children, or people walking on water. Prayer has the ability to alter physical properties and therefore create things and events that cannot be explained by the laws of nature. If we are stumped when trying to explain how this happens, it is because we lack the basic understanding that everything that is physical is a conception of that which is not physical (Source). Arguing that physical laws cannot change because they are static is like telling a sculptor they can no longer change the shape of a clay sculpture that they are in the eternal process of sculpting. Therefore, if we address a problem on the level of that which is not physical (Source), it is as good as rewriting the concept of this world.

Prayer can take many forms. It can take the form of an incantation, grace, a hymn, the giving of thanks, a confession, a chant, a moment of silence, an act of devotion, or even a simple, heartfelt request. No matter what form it takes, it is a conscious, deliberate opening up to receiving Source itself. Prayer causes a person to focus on their connection to Source. Whatever you focus on will come to be.

The prayer we are all most familiar with is the request form of prayer, which is the subject of many miracles as well as many disappointments. There is no inherent problem with request prayer. There is, however, often an inherent problem of focus. People can become very discouraged with Source when they feel they have been praying and their prayers have not been answered. But Source answers prayers every single time. It answers prayers by virtue of how it answers everything. It answers by virtue of where your focus lies. A person may pray all the days of their life and do it from a space of feeling inadequate. They pray from the prostrated ignorance of the fact that they are not separate from Source. In that unworthiness, a person cannot fully receive anything they ask for. The focus is not on the blissful having of it, it is on the justified absence of it.

A person cannot experience their own power from the standpoint of being unable to acknowledge that power. You can only ever benefit from fully trusting and letting go to Source. You cannot ever benefit from the thought that you are separate from Source, less than Source, and powerless to change conditions in your life. It takes some deep self-observation and honesty to realize where your focus actually is. Many people think their focus is on what they want when it is really on the antithesis of what they want.

The following represents a harsh example, however, it is a necessary one to illustrate this point. A parent with a sick child may be praying every day in these words: "Please don't let my child die." That parent may not understand that prayer is no exception to the fact that (as was discussed in chapter 3) there is no vibrational anti-note within the universe. The focus in this statement is on death and the extreme fear of and resistance to *it*.

The person praying does not feel relieved. They do not feel as though they trust the child will get better. The person feels desperation and grief. Therefore, the prayer is often answered directly by the death of the child by virtue of the parent's request made through focus on death. This request is obviously not intentional. The death of this child is no one's fault. It is simply a match to both the child and the parent's focus.

The way to make a prayer offer you a miracle is to believe it. Believe it will go the way you want it to go. Put yourself in the feeling state of knowing the relief of Source amassing all ingredients necessary to make your request come true for you. See it as having happened already. If your focus is truly on the full realization of what you have requested, it must come to be. It can be no other way than this. It is a universal law that supersedes any physical law you have taught yourself to believe. Your entire life can be a miracle if you can simply learn to believe before you see.

CHAPTER 11
DESIGNING YOUR PERFECT LIFE

Source is bliss. Abundant bliss, infinite bliss.
In bliss we are in complete knowledge of Source.
It is the feeling of connection to that which we truly are.
And so, make bliss—and nothing else—your everyday ambition.
Make bliss the mission of your life
and you will know Source from this day forward.

Talking to the people of the earth today, it becomes immediately obvious that we all prioritize different things. One person may prioritize attaining money, one might prioritize finding a lover, and one might prioritize being with their children. It would be easy to then assume that we have different motivations for our priorities. This is where we are wrong.

The reason people feel like they must prioritize money is because they think they would find happiness in having money. The reason people feel like they must prioritize finding a lover is because they think they would find happiness in having a lover. The reason people feel like they must prioritize being with their children is that they think they would find happiness in being with their children. In fact, the only motivation for anything we do is the idea that it will make us feel better. With this knowledge, there is no better reason to stop downplaying the importance of happiness and cut to the chase by making our number one priority happiness itself.

Most people seek their bliss, thinking that if they accomplish certain goals, attain certain possessions, and are appreciated and loved by others, they will attain bliss. The truth is that we attain bliss when we lay down the goals, possessions, and opinions of others and make our single and only career, goal, and purpose that of bliss. All else will fall in behind it. However, many of us are so cut off from the concept of our bliss that we do not even know what that means to us. We are cut off from really knowing ourselves. We seek the answer to what our bliss really is. It is different for everyone. The key to designing your life the way you want it to be is to know yourself.

The door to our true nature is unlocked by cultivating awareness. The term awareness is used a great deal, but it is difficult to find a unanimous definition for it. For the sake of the context in which it is used here, awareness means an objective, observant, cognizant form of knowledge that is born of expanded perceptive recognition. If we can peel away the layers of external things and defenses we have added to ourselves that we have then mistakenly identified as our actual selves, we are left with awareness of our essence. This will bring us beyond the limiting mechanics of our separate personalities so we can experience who we really are.

Awareness is not the same as focusing on what is so that you get more of what is and are condemned to repeating what is. Instead, it is more like waking up. Awareness is waking up from a reality you are creating by default because you have not chosen to switch into an "objective" enough view to realize your control. Awareness is what happens when you have lived and defined your life inside the parameters of an intellectual box because it is all you think about and all you see—only to shift your thoughts and suddenly see that more exists outside the parameters of that box you previously thought was the horizon of reality. Awareness is the ultimate observation. It is a state outside the thinking mind where you no longer identify with what you are observing. In that objectivity, instead of what you are observing having control over you, you now hold the power to take yourself off of autopilot in your actions and reactions.

In order to make positive changes, we must be able to catch ourselves in the act, which is a recognition born of awareness. Often we behave according to the dictates of our personality. We do not understand that this is a choice and therefore, we operate out of habit. When we are able to notice things like what we are doing now, how we are feeling now, what we like and dislike now, who we are now, and how all of it is serving us in the big picture of things in a state of honesty, without judgment- our old patterns will fall away, and we can live a life of our own choosing. This process of coming into awareness can be difficult. Initially, the recognition of where we are and what we are doing may make us feel ashamed, embarrassed, or vulnerable. But if you are able at that point to not give in to the negative urge to shut down or distract yourself away from that feeling, you will begin to feel the "you" which is beyond your identity in this life. It will feel like an essence that is more real and substantial—an essence that is very aware of your surroundings as well as the part of yourself that is wise, passionate, and patient as well as loving. This essence is who you really are.

The real you is a "feeling" place instead of a thing that is quantifiable, so it can only ever be experienced instead of intellectualized. Your true nature is unquantifiable.

Your real self is unquantifiable essence. Worldly things or accoutrements such as personality and material desires are not at the core of happiness, but they are helpful to identify in the process of awareness. They are integral to the knowledge of oneself. The key to the perfect answer of who you are as well as what constitutes your bliss is, of course, none other than the perfect question. Instead of asking negative questions that add to your powerlessness, such as "What is wrong with me?" start asking questions that lend to you creating the picture of your life the way you want it to be. That picture is who you really are. The answer to these questions will evolve throughout your life—just as you evolve throughout your life.

That is how it was intended to be.

A collection of questions you can keep coming back to throughout your life that will help you shape the picture of you is provided below. It is best to take out a pen and paper and write the answer down once you come to it. You can answer all of them or just the ones you are drawn to at the time.

- ☐ Do I realize that it is okay to not have all the answers?
- ☐ Do I realize that the point of life is to ask questions?
- ☐ What is the best question I think I could ask myself right now?
- ☐ Why is that the best question I can think to ask right now?
- ☐ How I think my life will improve once I find the answer to that question?
- ☐ What do I like most about myself?
- ☐ Why is this what I like most about myself?
- ☐ How do I feel, in general, about my life right now?
- ☐ Why do I feel this way?
- ☐ When did I begin to feel this way?
- ☐ Do I realize that it was a decision, either conscious or subconscious, to feel this way?
- ☐ Do I realize that the way I feel can change?
- ☐ Do I realize that the thoughts I think can change?

- ☐ Do I realize that I have the ability to think whatever thoughts I choose to think because the power I have in life is focus?
- ☐ What thought do I most want to think about myself?
- ☐ Why do I want to think this thought about myself?
- ☐ What thought do I want to think most about the world?
- ☐ Why do I want to think this thought about the world?
- ☐ What is the best thought I could think right now to change the way I feel for the better—even a little bit?
- ☐ What are my greatest talents and abilities?
- ☐ Do I think I have these abilities for a reason?
- ☐ Would it feel good to be able to use these abilities on a daily basis to benefit myself and others?
- ☐ Am I using these abilities on a daily basis already? If so, how does that feel to me?
- ☐ Can I think of any ways I could utilize my greatest talents and abilities?
- ☐ What is my most important goal in life right now?
- ☐ Why is this my most important goal?
- ☐ Are there any opportunities waiting for me that I could take right now to realize that goal?
- ☐ Why is it the best opportunity?
- ☐ How do I feel when I think about this opportunity?
- ☐ Do I feel worthy?
- ☐ Do I realize that worth has nothing to do with what I do or what I have done?
- ☐ What thought could I think right now to help myself feel worthy?
- ☐ What could I do right now to help myself feel worthy?
- ☐ Do I love myself?
- ☐ Do I realize that the most important thing in life is to love myself?
- ☐ Do I realize that the Source that is my more expansive self loves me unconditionally?
- ☐ Do I realize that I deserve love?
- ☐ What thought could I think right now that could show love to myself?
- ☐ What could I do right now to show love to myself?
- ☐ Do I treat myself as well as I want to treat others?
- ☐ What can I think that will allow me to treat myself as well as I want to treat others?
- ☐ What can I do that will mean I am treating myself as well as I want to treat others?

- What are my main motivations in my life?
- Do I want these to be my main motivations?
- What do I think would be the best motivation to have in my life?
- How can I think differently to make these my main motivations?
- What can I do differently in my life to live according to these motivations?
- What thought can I think each day to make my life more pleasurable?
- What can I do each day to make my life more pleasurable?
- What are my favorite things to think about life?
- What are my favorite things to do?
- How could I maximize my enjoyment of these things?
- Do I realize that if I am doing these things in my mind, I will feel as though I am actually doing them?
- What steps can I take to do more of these things?
- What thought can I think about myself that will bring out the best in me?
- What can I do to bring out the best in myself?
- What thought can I think about others that will bring out the best in them?
- What can I do to bring out the best in others?
- How do I identify what to do on a daily basis?
- What would be a better way to decide what to do on a daily basis?
- Who is the most important person in my life?
- Why is this person the most important person in my life?
- What do I love most about this person?
- What quality does this person bring out in me that I like about myself?
- Do I count on and trust myself first in life?
- Why should I count on and trust myself first?
- Is that answer in line with how I want to think and who I want to be?
- What thoughts could I think that would help me count on and trust myself every day?
- What is the time that stands out to me in my life that I proved I could count on and trust myself?
- What quality do I admire most in others?
- Do I want this quality to be my own?
- Why do I want this quality to be my own?
- Do I realize that I can have any quality I want to have?
- What would be the best thoughts I could think to adopt this quality?

- What could I do in my life to adopt this quality?
- What quality of mine is most beneficial to me?
- What quality of mine that I have already is the most beneficial to others?
- Who can benefit most from what I have to offer?
- When am I most blissful?
- When am I at my best?
- What thoughts can I think that help me to be at my best?
- How can I create opportunities to be at my best?
- Where is my favorite place?
- Why is this my favorite place?
- Do I realize that if I visualize being in this place, it will feel as though I am actually there?
- Is there a way that I could look for or create the things I love about that place where I am now?
- Where might I find the people who will best bring out my health and happiness?
- What is my best source of inspiration?
- If I was to meet an alien from another planet, what would I say was the part I loved most about my physical life on earth?
- What thoughts are most beneficial to my self-confidence?
- What actions are the most beneficial to my self-confidence?
- What is the most loving action I think a person could take?
- What is the thing I value most about my home?
- Why do I value that thing?
- What do I value most about what I do on a daily basis?
- Why do I value that the most?
- What do I value most about my body?
- Why do I value this about my body?
- What do I value the most about my mind?
- Why do I value this about my mind?
- What do I value most about the life I have lived up until this point?
- Why do I value this the most?
- What is the thing I value most about myself spiritually?
- Why do I value this the most?
- What do I value most about feeling loved?
- Why is this what I value most about feeling loved?
- What is my greatest fantasy?

- ☐ Why is this my greatest fantasy?
- ☐ Do I realize that there is nothing I can't do, have, or be?
- ☐ Do I realize I deserve this fantasy to be true for me?
- ☐ What can I think of on a daily basis that will help me feel as though this is going to be true for me?
- ☐ What can I do on a daily basis to help this become a reality for me?
- ☐ Does it feel good to think about doing these things?
- ☐ Why does it make me feel good to think about doing these things?
- ☐ If I could pick one way to maximize my enjoyment of life in the next year, what would it be?
- ☐ What do I value most about friendship in general?
- ☐ Why do I value that the most?
- ☐ What was the best day of my life?
- ☐ What made it the best day of my life?
- ☐ What did I learn that I wanted in life from that day?
- ☐ Have I followed that desire?
- ☐ How could I best follow that desire—right here and now?
- ☐ What do I value most about my health?
- ☐ Why do I value this the most?
- ☐ What thoughts could I think about my health that would help me feel healthier?
- ☐ What could I do in life that would lead to me feeling healthier?
- ☐ When I see the word purpose, what thought comes to my mind?
- ☐ Why does that thought come up?
- ☐ How does that thought feel to me?
- ☐ What thoughts could I think that would make me feel good in relation to the idea of purpose?
- ☐ Do I realize that my purpose is being fulfilled, here and now?
- ☐ What do I think my life's purpose might be?
- ☐ Why might this be my life's purpose?
- ☐ Does this make me feel good?
- ☐ Can I give myself permission to change my idea of what my life's purpose is?
- ☐ How can I better put myself in the position of allowing inspiration instead of forcing actions so that I can just flow easily into my purpose?
- ☐ What do I think about death?
- ☐ Does it feel good to think about death in this way?
- ☐ What thoughts can I think to help me feel better about death?

- Why would these thoughts make me feel better about death?
- Can I give myself permission to believe these new thoughts?
- In what ways do I believe in myself the most?
- How do I imagine the world around me would change if everyone was following their own happiness?
- What one belief is hindering me the most in my life?
- Am I ready to give this belief up?
- Where did this belief come from?
- Do I realize it is my choice to keep believing this?
- How do I decide whether something is right or accurate?
- Do I want this to be how I define what is right or accurate?
- How do I want to decide whether something is right or accurate?
- What thoughts can I think that will lead me to live by that definition of what is right or accurate?
- What thought comes to mind when I picture my idea of a happy life?
- With that in mind, what one thing could I think right now that would help my life be more joyous and free from struggle?
- If I start thinking about what a more joyous life would look like, what one thing comes to mind that I feel inspired to eliminate from my life that will help my life be more joyous and free from struggle?
- How does it make me feel when I think of being free of this thing?
- When I think about what a more joyous life would look like to me, what one thing comes to mind that I could add to my life to enhance my enjoyment?
- What am I the most committed to?
- Do I want to be committed to this thing?
- What do I want to be committed to?
- How could I best commit myself to these things?
- What are some things that are positive about the situation in my life that are the most displeasing to me right now?
- What are some of the traits I most admire about the person who is the most difficult for me to love right now?
- What are some of the amazing benefits I got out of the pain I have experienced previously in my life?
- What am I the most grateful for?
- In what ways could I help myself focus on what I am most grateful for on a daily basis?
- How do I imagine this would make me feel differently than I feel now?

- What do I most want to get out of life?
- Why is this what I want to get out of life?
- What thoughts can I think that would help me feel as though I am getting these things out of life?
- What can I do differently to fully realize these things in my life?
- What thoughts am I thinking that are creating the feelings I have in life?
- What thoughts do I want to think instead?
- What thoughts do I think that are creating the good feelings I have in life?
- What is a personal achievement I want to have in my life?
- What is the real reason I want this achievement?
- Do I like the reason I want this achievement?
- What are the thoughts I could think that would make me feel as though this achievement is inevitable?
- What do I care about most deeply?
- When I think of something I definitely don't want in my life, how does that help me to know that I do want?
- What are some ways I could find to focus on what I do want?
- If I had one year to live, what would I do to make the most bliss come of that last year of life?
- How could I better live my life so that I am living every year like I only have one year left?
- What is my favorite memory?
- Why is this my favorite memory?
- How do I want my life to be more like this memory?
- What are some things I could do to allow this to happen?
- What things fill me with passion?
- Why do they fill me with passion?
- What needs and wants are already being fulfilled in my life?
- Am I the person I want to be?
- What kind of person do I want to be?
- In what ways am I already the person I want to be?
- What thoughts could I think that would bring me closer to being that person?
- What things could I do that would bring me closer to being that person?
- Does it feel good to think about thinking and doing those things?

- [ ] What are the benefits I will gain by thinking thoughts and doing things that will make me feel good?
- [ ] What do I love about today?
- [ ] How can I make the best use of this moment?

The questions you could ask yourself to become a better energetic match to the way you want your life to be are endless. Some of them may seem redundant, but you will find that even in the course of sitting down to write your answers, the answers you have previously written down may change. This process is meant to help you identify and hone in on your deepest truth of the life you intend for yourself—which may not be what you immediately think it is.

It may also be helpful to make a list of all of your favorite things and then make another list to match it explaining why those are your favorite things. You can list as many things as you would like, such as your favorite color, food, animal, person, time period, or movie—the sky is the limit. You will come to know yourself very well when you ask those questions. If you ask why, you will expose the genuine reasons behind what you think. In that exposure, you can decide if you like those reasons—at which point, you can focus on changing your thoughts into the thoughts you want to think.

This may seem trivial to a person who has been stuck in the physical dimension for a long time. But everything you see around you originated as a thought. If you change your thoughts, you will change your life. The revision of your entire life through your thoughts can come of this simple act of self-questioning.

CHAPTER 12
THE POSITIVE OF NEGATIVE

Here in this suffering, all previous beliefs are called into question.
They are consumed in the fire sparked and
fueled by our own illusion.
The pain becomes the ashes we are now entombed in.
It is only when we find ourselves
at this most imprisoned of junctures
that we emerge again, the phoenix of our very life
which is ever so much more beautiful than the last one.

We do not need to live our lives in the constant process of running away from and pushing against the negative. You do not need to see it as the enemy. If you do see it as the enemy, it is an enemy that comes into its power when you run away from it. If you do see it as an enemy, it gets stronger the more you wage war against it. If you address it instead as the comrade it could be, its power would dwindle. At that point, you could use it to your benefit and see it as a gift—and better yet, an opportunity.

This subject has been touched on previously in this book, but it is a subject that warrants its own chapter, because it is a skill that is integral in finding bliss. Living a positive life does not mean putting a coat of varnish over negativity, but rather, it means learning how to spin in the direction of what is negative and take its power away by seeing it for what it really is. You then realize that you have the power of focus to turn in the opposite direction of it. It is also more than that. It is realizing that the entire purpose of negativity in your life is to help you discern what its opposite is. It helps you discern what you want and what the picture of your perfect universe would look like.

If you have ever met a person who has birthed their new, blissful self out of extreme adversity, they will tell you they would never take the adversity back. There is nothing like the blackest black to show you the whitest white. People with the darkest experiences often have the comparison necessary to birth the happiest lives. In fact, many decide before birth to specifically look to come into a birth or childhood environment that will set them up for just the kind of comparison that they know will help them to further evolve themselves, and Source at large, into the furthermost kind of bliss and oneness.

The entire purpose of negativity is to exist as a comparison to use in order to shape your future life, and Source, into the exactness of what you want it to be. If this society wants something, just like people wanted the ability to connect to each other through technological means, that desire will be fulfilled eventually. When it is fulfilled, that new state that is achieved will come endowed with a brand new set of negatives, such as the fact that society will now be so dependent on technology for connection, that people within it feel no interpersonal connection. Those new negatives are what serve to help us know what is even better than what we previously wanted. This is not for it to be back the way it was, but for us to pull even more into this picture of what we want our evolved selves and universe to be- like a society that enjoys both interpersonal and technological connection in perfect balance. We live in a time when most of us have been told continually that "you can't have your cake and eat it, too." But the truth of this universe is, and always has been, that having your cake and eating it too is the entire point of your life. The only thing preventing you from it is the limiting belief that this universe is one of finite boundaries and so there must be give and take. There is no such thing as give and take unless you believe there to be. You do not want that kind of physical life. Since you are the one creating this physical life, you can change it to be whatever you want it to be.

Negativity not only helps you to shape your life the way you want it to be, but it also helps you shape yourself the way you want yourself to be. It works even if you have not formed the picture of what you want to be yet. It does this by showing you to yourself in plain view. If you are practicing a way of behaving and thinking in this life, you will see the immediate physical aftermath of that in manifested form. If those ways of behaving and thinking are not an energetic vibration that finds resonance with that of your higher self and what you truly want, you will look at them and call them negative. If you push against them and run away from them hard enough, you will realize pushing and running doesn't work. You will have no choice but to change the way you think and behave, and in doing so, you will have caught up to your wants. You will come closer to your bliss.

The question is this: was the negative manifestation a detriment or an extreme benefit to the life you have lived? When you are in the middle of it, holding on to the illusion that it is possible to be a victim of anything, you may say it is a detriment. But you will know, the more you get in touch with your transcendental mind and your truth, that there is no such thing as a victim. The negative benefits you more than anything else in your evolution and the evolution of all that is. All that is positive and all that is negative is just a reflection of what we have been thinking and being as well as what we are thinking and what we are now. What has been is gone, and what is, changes at an interval that a human mind cannot grasp, like less than seconds, or even less than milliseconds.

A big part of the ingredient to you not living the life you want to live is rooted in the fact that we all have negative beliefs or thoughts that are on a repetitive loop which have made themselves so much a part of our physical lives, we regard them as truth—or even worse, we become completely unaware of what they are. The term that has been used for this over the years is a negative, self-limiting core belief. These beliefs—which are only as true as you believe them to be—are felt by you as rational only because in believing them, they have become manifested in the physical form, at which point you believed them more, at which point they manifested more, at which point you believed them more … and this spiral goes on.

In human society, we call anything rational that you can see in the form of the physical proof. The problem arises from the fact that physical proof is only the result of what we or someone else has previously thought. It is the core beliefs that are the most practiced and energetic vibrations in your life. Though they are often covert, they are the most dominant, and therefore are the ones that are creating the most in your life. These beliefs are the reason your life looks like it does now. It is beneficial for the negative core beliefs to be found and then starved of attention as you begin to replace them with different beliefs. It can be a bit like hunting an elusive target, although once you hit it and see that it is not a useful belief for you to hold, you will feel a kind of sweet relief that you have never known.

When you come into a situation in which you experience strong negative emotion, you have the absolute perfect opportunity to find your self- limiting negative core beliefs. You can do this by chasing every statement you have with the perfect question. Two questions that seem to work very well are "Why would that be a bad thing?" and "What would it mean if that were true?" For example, if you get into a situation where you are afraid, such as being very afraid of failing at something- the statement, "I am afraid I will fail" is not the core belief—it is an emotional reaction to the actual core belief. You can find the core belief by asking, "Why would that be a bad thing?" The answer may be, "I will look stupid." You then ask yourself, "Why would that be a bad thing?" the answer may be, "Other people will think I'm stupid." Ask, "Why would that be a bad thing?" The answer may be, "I will be rejected." Then ask, "What would that mean to me if that were true?" The answer may be, "I will feel worthless and I will be alone." Then ask, "Why would that be a bad thing?" The answer may be, "I will never be happy if I am alone." So, "I will never be happy if I am alone" is the core belief in this example. You have chased down the root of why you are afraid of failing.

Often there is more than one layer to a core belief. If you examine the sequence of statements, it is easy to see many core beliefs operating besides the end result, or main core belief that you come to. In the example above, the person above not only has the belief that they cannot be happy if they are alone, but also that "if someone else believes I am stupid, then I am worthless." From that, you can infer another core belief, which is "if someone thinks I am smart, I have worth," and yet another core belief, which is that "whether I fail or succeed is determined by others." The answers will be different for everyone. Another person could have the very same fear of failing, with a very different core belief behind it. When you find a core belief within yourself, the belief itself may often sound totally illogical to you—even ridiculous. This is a good thing, because that makes it easier to start to think things that are the opposite. It is easier to talk oneself out of a belief that seems ridiculous than one that makes sense. You must realize though that even though it can seem ridiculous, it has been a belief of yours. It is a belief that has rendered physical manifestations to match it, so it is a core belief that is affecting you greatly and preventing you from your bliss. We must get past the surface of thoughts and feelings, as well as immediate reactions to find beliefs, as well as know ourselves and become the people we want to be. Even though it seems that your previous experiences make you a certain way by default, the truth you will find once you reclaim the freedom that is already yours is that you are only the byproduct of as much of your previous experiences as you choose to be.

Once you find these self-limiting core beliefs, you can look at those and define from them what you truly want to believe. This is a process you can call a turnabout. You must change your point of view in order to change your core beliefs. You can do this by first identifying what your core belief is and then finding out with the use of that awareness what its antithesis is. You use the awareness of what makes you unhappy to do a turnabout and find what would make you happy. You use your awareness of what is undesirable for you to find out what is desirable to you. This process of turning about can be used in any circumstance of which you feel negative emotion, not just with regards to core beliefs. The word turnabout is just a way of reminding yourself to use what you see as negative as a basis to help you find what is positive, or that which is 180 degrees in the opposite direction of it.

When using the above example, if your core belief is, "I will not be happy if I am alone," then you can add a new desire to your life which can become a reality if you let your higher self show you the *how* of it. The new desire may sound like, "I want to be happy regardless of whether I am with company or alone," or "I want to feel and know that my sense of worth is dependent on how I feel instead of anyone else's opinion of me," or "I want to feel like I have succeeded regardless of what others think." In order to fulfill these desires, you simply have to pick thoughts you do already believe that support what you want to believe, such as, "Other people have learned how to be happy when they aren't around other people, which means I could do that too," or "If a baby has worth, I have worth, and I have not lost any worth since I was a baby, because I am an ever-evolving being who always has potential energy." You can begin to talk yourself into a higher energetic vibration by finding thoughts to support the beliefs you want to have. Starve the negative beliefs by not feeding them the negative thoughts that support the belief you are in the habit of thinking.

That which we call negativity does not have to turn into suffering. It only turns into suffering when we are unaware of the negative beliefs within us, and when we get stuck in a cycle of focusing incessantly on the problem rather than the solution. Then our focus is so negative that it is all we see in this world. It turns into suffering when we think we are not the ones with the power or ability to change it- when we fear it, and when we wage war against what we see that is negative instead of simply lending all our mental and physical energies to what we see as positive in the situation, as well as the positive that that negativity is helping us identify as something we want. In other words, suffering only comes from not following the north star of our emotions—thereby continuing to reinforce a negative energetic vibration within ourselves. Suffering has become natural to humankind—a thing some people see as a sort of inevitability to our existence. But suffering does not have to be inevitable to our existence. Whether it is or not is in your hands. It all rests in how you see negativity and what your response to negativity is.

CHAPTER 13
THE SCOPE OF STILLNESS
AND THE FREEDOM
OF FORGIVENESS

Here, the now is always changing...
changing always into itself.
The new face of now is still itself, and itself is still.
The now is a forever genre of emptiness containing everything that is,
even everything that ever was.
At every moment, you stand on alien ground,
presented ceaselessly the opportunity to become new with it.
Stop dragging the shackles of what was forward with you.
Too long they have sounded their iron clang across your years.
You are blameless, as everything is blameless.
Let it go,
for those who deliver themselves the life sentence of injustice
sleep pressed up against the coarse and bitter bars
of their own self-constructed jail cells.
While all the universe is yelling, let forgiveness be your key.

There is no substitute for stillness. Without stillness, nothing can free us from the shackles and waves of our limited, three-dimensional experiences. To begin on this internal journey of finding the stillness within you, it may be necessary to free yourself from the bondage of where you are by first making peace with it. Instead of keeping yourself chained to the state you are in now by being frustrated that you are not yet where you want to be, acknowledge that it is just the state you are in and that everything is temporary. We must slow down in order to observe our current state and place. A good way to do this is to create times, or even schedule entire days of inaction. In the beginning of this journey, we need to be okay with simply being instead of doing. It is hard to do nothing, especially in this physical world that is addicted to the drug of action. You think that when you are not doing something, you are wasting your time. But your time exists for the sole reason for you to be, not for you to do. The fertile ground for inspired action is to first be. We yell at ourselves that we must not just sit there and that we must get up and do something. This is not the first step to happiness.

Happiness begins when you begin the practice of telling yourself the reverse statement—"don't just get up and do something, sit there." If you do this for a time, you will come in the beginning to realize that you are not the one who has control over your action. Just like an addiction, your action has control over you. It will pull at you. You will feel the sensation of withdrawal from it when you try to just *be* without doing. You must simply remember that being constantly busy will not satisfy you. It is the reason for a good deal of suffering. We are afraid of what will be in the room with us if we stop being busy. When we become still and just be, we are suddenly in the present moment with all of our fears, insecurities, anger, pain, and boredom. We are suddenly in the room with the very things we are running from with our constant action. But any action that is made from a negative emotional place will cause manifestations that only reinforce the state we were in to begin with. It is only in the stopping of action that we are still enough to realize where we are. It is only when we stop running from the fears, insecurities, anger, pain, and boredom that they cease to have power over us. They begin to dissolve. The same resistance you had to the thing you are running away from is the fuel it is using to stay alive in you. Your resistance against it is actually your focus upon it. You were not acting out of focus of what you did want. You were acting out of focus of what you didn't want—and what you didn't want got bigger.

Observance is true awareness. What pulls us out of observant awareness and back into the trappings of our habits so that we remain prisoners of them is the fact that we have not learned to observe and let go. Observing and then letting go is one of the most important skills to acquire in the quest to create positive change, as is knowledge of stillness. We must learn to observe what is in the here and now, both outside and inside of ourselves. We must also observe what pulls us away from the here and now. We must not condemn or criticize what we uncover through our observations. Most importantly, we must not push against it in frustration, thinking that attempting to forcibly change it will eradicate it. Contrary to what your unhealthy ego-self would have you believe, it is actually not your purpose in life to forcibly repair or change yourself. Positive change is the result of focus upon what you want, not the result of focus upon what you do not want.

The idea that we must fix ourselves or what is around us (including others) is a central trapping of illusion. You are not playing perpetual catch-up with a god that stands in judgment of you and has a perfect ideal for you that you must live up to. If you have become this type of god for yourself, you are standing in the way of the natural flow of your own happiness. It can be very difficult to transition into the state of observance and letting go because you live in a society that you have acclimated to in this time and space. This society has influenced you with unhealthy ideas that you have accepted such as "I must do better, achieve more, work harder, or be different that I am." In truth, the negativity of society (in most cases, the whole of your early education at home and at school) is one of constant indoctrination that you must be more successful, more desirable, more accomplished—you *must* be more. The underlying message in all of this is that you are not successful, you are not desirable, you are not accomplished—you are not enough.

You are also influenced to believe that success is determined by those outside of you who are observing you. This way of thinking goes against the entire way this universe was set up. It is a formula that has given rise to much desire for freedom, happiness, and unconditional love. But as is the way of it, this formula has given rise to these desires because it is a formula for misery. This way of thinking makes it so we hold ourselves apart from positive change because we hold our deficiencies as the object of our constant attention—which means we will only manifest more of that into our reality. What enables you to change is realizing that it is not that you should change because you are not loveable or worthy if you do not. Instead, you want to change because you know that the change would lend to your happiness, and in return, it would lend to the happiness of all that is. What enables that change is not haranguing and punishing ourselves for what we observe in ourselves. What enables change is that we can observe and recognize all things in ourselves as well as realize that all things are temporary snapshots in time. In that recognition, we can let go of them, thereby releasing what we do not want by instead focusing on the new picture of what we want to observe in ourselves instead.

The same goes for things you observe outside yourself. Anything you observe outside yourself is simply a reflection of what is inside you, so it is best to address observation of your inner self first. That being said, when you observe something outside yourself, you can still let go of it so as to focus on the picture of what you really want instead. This will feel as though you are letting the other person off the hook, when what you are really doing is letting yourself off the hook. You no longer need the outside thing you are observing to change in order to feel better. You are recognizing that you had the choice to keep yourself snagged on the hook, using what you observe as your excuse to feel bad or simply let go of the hook and swim in the direction of what you would prefer to observe— even if this means simply imagining what you would prefer to observe. You can drop habits that have spanned a lifetime with this simple act of observation and letting go. When you are cultivating awareness of the habits you have instead of falling prey to the trappings of them, you have accessed the *you* that is outside the ego. You are experiencing your life through the eyes of the inner observer, which is your true essential self. You are not only experiencing your life from the three-dimensional format in which you identify with intensely, but you are also witnessing your life in a transcendental, observant way as you experience it. This observer is your eternal self that is experienced through the stillness in the spaces between the observation, the release of that observation, and the coming of the new observation. Observing and letting go is the first step to stillness.

If you realize that everything is temporary, the present moment you are in takes on a quality that is quite beautiful. There are many practices set up around the concept of the present moment. In truth, the present moment is all there is. All that exists from the past is what part of the past you have made a part of your current thoughts. All that exists of the future is what part of the future you have made part of your current thoughts now. It is only when you slow down to a state of stillness that you can even experience the perspective of Source. It is only in stillness that you can experience what you have created through your past thoughts. It is awareness of now. There is no time in the now, because this measurement we call *now* is always changing. It can never be a linear thing. It is only in stillness that you can even observe the thoughts you are thinking.

Your thinking mind is a tool for your observing mind. All tools need rest to function at their highest potential. All tools must also be laid down in order for the tool wielder to realize that they are separate from the tool itself. Once you become the observer of the thoughts you are thinking, you no longer identify with them, and they lose their power to move you into action. This is important, because the only point of power you have is control of your thoughts—and the only point from which you are able to change your thoughts is now. Discomfort dissolves in the now. You cannot be completely in the now and resist the now at the same time. Everything simply is—without judgment. Without the idea of how something ought to be, how it is, is just how it is, and there is no discordant energetic vibration in that.

Source flows into everything you do if your focus is completely in doing it. It is the pure state of allowing. When you are in this pure state, even things you see as unpleasant are pleasant. A good example is doing dishes. When you are doing dishes, open your attention to feel everything in the now—not what you'd rather be doing, not what happened a minute ago, not judgment about what you're doing, such as "I don't like how hot the water is." Just observe the feeling of the water running over your hands. Hear the sounds of the dishes clanking against the side of the sink when you move them. Observe the way it looks, feels, and sounds to move the sponge over them. If your mind strays, don't condemn it—just bring it back to what you are doing in the now. When the dishes are done, you will notice you had no sensation of time. You also did not wish for the dishes to be done before they were done. You were so in the process, you were not identified with the outcome of the process. You will also find yourself in a good mood. You were not thinking of what you wanted to be doing instead, and so it didn't feel like a chore. You were doing what you intended to do in coming into physical life—experiencing regardless of what the experience was.

We never really realize to what extent we do not experience the life we are living until we stop and find stillness. There is an ancient practice in eastern culture called mindful eating. It is a practice that is of extreme benefit to the practice of stillness. Eating is an integral part of life for all living creatures in the physical dimension. It is an opportunity to feel what it is to be alive. We take it for granted, like most things we have made repetitive in our lives. However, instead of treating food as an escape from negative emotion, an enemy, or a necessity that errs on the side of a burden, it is possible to see it as an avenue of joy and experiencing *being*.

When it comes time for you to eat, you can sit down with whatever you have chosen to eat. Without thinking of anything else or having conversation with anyone else, you can start to experience the food as it is—what it looks, feels, and smells like—and then slowly, you can experience what it tastes like. Fully focus on the sensation so that the food is all that you notice. After a time, you can start to think about the ingredients in the food, where they came from, and the process they underwent in order to make it from their origin to your plate, the hands it passed through, and the energy that went into making it. You can try to search for the flavor of the sunshine, the earth, and the rain that went into the food—they are all still a part of what you are eating. You can think of any and all aspects of the food itself. You can find thankfulness for it. You can be in the present moment with it. You can be its observer. You will be surprised at how much of the experience of eating you completely miss on a regular basis just because of a lack of attention to it in the now. This, and any state of being in the present moment is a state in which the ego self does not exist. Because it does not exist, it is not interfering and you are free of discordant energetic vibration. You are letting health and bliss in. It is inevitable that in the physical life, we are going to come to desires.

This is the cause of evolution, which is the point to life. If a person could live, however, in the present moment like this as much as possible, they would fully allow the magnetic pull of Source toward those desires and therefore would get there with no effort at all—and very quickly. We would be in the process of letting ourselves live by our higher selves instead of trying to take control and put forth effort to live. Once you have found stillness and made peace with where you are, it becomes much easier to begin to use the tool of your mind to create and find resonance with your creations through deliberately maintaining an energetic vibration of bliss.

Just as stillness is the practice of making peace with where you are so as to experience the eternal presence behind where you are—which subsequently releases you from the bondage keeping you from bliss—forgiveness is the practice of making peace with where you were, thereby releasing you from the bondage keeping you from bliss. Forgiveness is much like setting a prisoner free only to discover that you were the prisoner all along. Quite often in life, when we do not make immediate harmony of things that cause us to suffer, they become wounds of the mind—wounds we carry with us in our consciousness and sub consciousness every day.

The pain becomes like shackles we are so used to living with that we do not even realize we have the power to take them off.

Forgiveness is a complete release of the energetic vibrations that the energetic vibration of joy. In true forgiveness, the negative emoti longer exists. It is a deep feeling of peace. And because of this, it is freed Often, simply for the sake of knowing the inherent goodness of forgiveness we try to rush ourselves into forgiveness when we have not yet changed the thoughts we are thinking about whatever we are trying to forgive. It can never happen this way. For example, when a person says, "I will forgive, but never forget," it is the very tone of captivity in that statement that lets you know true forgiveness has not become a part of them yet. True forgiveness is forgetfulness. It is not the forgetfulness we think of in terms of losing mental recollection of the past, because you may never forget what happened. Instead the recollection of it will not bring the negative emotions along with it anymore. In fact, you may hold a totally different emotion toward it—such as gratitude—for what it made possible in your life today.

It is that altered recollection that proves the memory does not hold you captive any longer. To say "I have forgiven" and not fully feel the peaceful freedom of it is to use the word forgiveness loosely without the full meaning of it. It is to try to convince ourselves to ignore, suppress, or gloss over a very deep wound. Under these conditions, the internal wound—just like a physical wound—will fester. We can get to the place of forgiveness at any second, but it is a process in every case. Upon being deeply hurt, in order to even come out of that powerless incapacity, a person may have to acknowledge the hurt and sadness and then get angry first before they can even venture into the vicinity of forgiveness. And this is okay. It is very important that we give ourselves permission to go through this process in order to avoid the trap of feeling guilty that we have not fully forgiven yet—on top of the terrible feelings of being hurt. When the time is right, it will not feel better to do anything other than forgive. And there is no one more important to forgive than ourselves.

In truth, forgiveness has nothing to do with anyone other than us.

Though it can feel very good to a receiving party, forgiveness is only ever about ourselves. Whether it is someone else we are forgiving or ourselves we are forgiving, forgiveness is only ever unilateral. We do not need the other person present in order to forgive them—or ourselves. The healing takes place within oneself alone. The feelings of resentment, guilt, and injustice that are present are entirely about our discordance with the Source within us. The thoughts we are thinking that have made it possible

on to manifest in our reality to begin with are not in
getic vibration of our higher self, so those emotions
that contradiction. Your higher self does not see
It does not see anything in a negative light. To
thing as injustice. Any thoughts that are aligned
points of view are not in line with your higher self and therefore
they are not in line with Source. Forgiveness is the process of shifting
thoughts in the direction of resonance with your higher self. It does not
take back anything—it is a release so that you can go forward. If we have
any pain in us at all, it means we have something to forgive.

Anything you give attention to will intensify, so, it may seem odd
that it would ever benefit a person to look backward toward something
negative. While it is best to turn completely in the direction of what you
want and what feels good by giving focus purely to that, at times we are so
out of touch with our own energetic vibration that we do not even realize
we have resentment still present within us. It becomes part of our daily
life and our identity. Often, we have ingrained beliefs that impede our
focus on the positive in the first place. This is when the process of turning
in the direction of the negative for the purpose of releasing is beneficial.
In this process, the purpose is not to dwell in the negative situation, but
rather to become aware of it and then immediately align with the solution
by mentally changing the situation into what you want it to be. In this
process, you are initiating these negative vibrations in order to experience
the conscious, deliberate shifting of them. You are causing them to shape-
shift with the power of your own focus. There are thousands of techniques
centered on forgiveness. Some of them may not speak to you, but others
you will find transforming. It is all about the process of finding what feels
good to you.

If you like, you can begin with this visualization of forgiveness. Sit
alone, as if in meditation, and focus on your breathing for a time. Then
set a timer for two minutes. In those two minutes, think of something
that made you feel very hurt that someone else said or did that you are
still holding on to the memory of. Remember how it felt, where you were,
and what you were thinking. Allow yourself to be taken completely back
into this space of pain. When the timer goes off, set it for five minutes.
During these five minutes, visualize yourself walking up to that person
and saying, "I forgive you." Tell them any healing thing you can think
of that lets them know that you understand the painful emotions they

were feeling that allowed them to act the way they acted or say the things they said. Imagine this person fully accepting the apology. Imagine them wanting it and just being afraid to ask for it. Imagine yourself embracing that person. Stay with this, creating the thought place of this reconciliation until the timer goes off.

Then set the timer for two minutes. During the two minutes, recall a time that you did or said something you regret doing—something you still carry the pain of having done. Recall the way it felt when you did it—where you were, who was there, and the pain on that person's face. Allow yourself to be taken back into that space of pain. When the timer goes off, set it for five minutes and for those five minutes imagine asking forgiveness from whomever you hurt. Imagine wanting it. Imagine the person giving it to you freely. Imagine them feeling joy in giving forgiveness to you. Imagine the pain going away completely as you give yourself over completely to the reconciliation, knowing it is all okay now. It is over. You are forgiven.

This time, when the timer goes off, without setting it again, imagine you forgiving yourself for this same action or thing you said. You can say to yourself, "I forgive you," "I know you are a loving person," or "I know you never meant to hurt anyone." Say anything to yourself that you need to hear in order to free yourself from your feelings of guilt or disappointment. Imagine hugging yourself. Imagine telling yourself that you understand why you did it. Let yourself know how much you believe in yourself. Maintain this visualization for as long as it takes for you to begin to feel a sense of peace, release, and even hopefulness. When you feel ready, open your eyes.

It may be easier for you to do this with someone else instead of alone. Another person can be the one to watch the time for you and verbally guide you through the different sections in this process that you may be afraid to initiate alone. This process can be very difficult. It can be like uncorking a dam that has been building up pressure for years. It can make you aware of your feelings of vulnerability. It can even make you break down—but breaking down will feel better than the pressure you were living with, because what you are in fact breaking down is everything that is blocking you from finding your bliss.

It may also be helpful to write a letter (no matter if the person is alive or dead), either offering someone forgiveness or asking for it from them. You can send this letter if you want to, or you can partake in a very cleansing practice of going somewhere (where there is no risk of anything catching fire) and burning the letter. You can watch the fire consume the words you have written, knowing everything you have said is being devoured by and becoming part of non-physical knowing. Let the fire pull away the pain in you as it pulls the words and the paper into itself.

It is very profound to write yourself a letter asking for your own forgiveness or giving yourself forgiveness and then burning it. Give yourself permission to experience the very strong emotional release that often accompanies this process. You can follow the intense release of such a practice by making use of the fertile ground of nonresistance that is present afterwards and focus strongly on something positive. For example, you can look deliberately for good memories, write affirmations, or write lists of positive aspects about your life right now.

True forgiveness is not a process of trying to make oneself resign to what is negative, which is often what it has been bastardized into. It is letting go of what is holding you back once you are aware of it so you can turn in the direction of bliss as well as discontinue carrying the past into the present. Every piece of release and bliss is found in the alteration of the point of view you are holding about a subject. If you remove yourself far enough from the limited point of view of pain, you will see that at the root of all things that are negative in this world is the physical fact that we are all nothing but the victims of victims. Remove yourself even farther than that, and you will see that there is no such thing as a victim. Victimhood is just a prison of illusion restricted to physical life—and forgiveness is the way out of it.

CHAPTER 14
THE PURSUIT OF
POSITIVE RESONANCE

Always in the narrow scope of adversity and
advantage can possibility for triumph be seen.
Success is always yours for the taking.
Joy is always yours for the taking.
They always have been, and they always will be.
The real value you hold in life is not in what cards
you have been dealt, but how you play them.
Your life can be a triumph in spite of any kind of adversity—
Or
Your life can be a tragedy in spite of every advantage.
Your freedom lies in the fact that it is your choice—
which way you create your life to be.

Your life can be a triumph in spite of any kind of adversity. The pursuit of positive resonance may feel difficult at first because training yourself in a way counter to what you have been habitually practicing for a very long time takes a bit of effort. Once you have made peace with where you are, it is true that the way to achieve bliss from wherever you are is to turn in the direction of what feels better to you—be it a thought, person, place, or thing—and think in that direction. Make what feels good your focus.

The single most valuable ingredient to holding a positive energetic resonance is that of thankfulness. The state of thankfulness I am talking about is not the one that you are probably familiar with. It is not the state of gratitude, which comes from a space of acute current awareness of what it is like to not have something. Gratitude is a bit like experiencing what is wanted with the feeling of what is not wanted still present. On an energetic level, it is not a pure energetic vibration, because it is not just the vibration of what is wanted, but it is also the vibration of its antithesis. Gratitude is what a person feels when they feel lucky to have something instead of realizing it is not about luck, but rather, it is something they have created. Gratitude keeps a person prisoner to the outside deliverance of that which they seek. It breeds guilt, a feeling of unworthiness or indebtedness, a fear of the possibility of losing what they have, a fear of going backward, and an unhealthy type of prostration.

The kind of thankfulness I am talking of is the energetic vibration of appreciation or admiration of what is. It is the pure vibration of focusing on the positive aspects of what is already in the present moment of your life and allowing the feeling of those aspects to envelop you completely.

Thankfulness in terms of appreciative notice is conscious acknowledgement and enjoyment of what you have received in the present moment as a result of finding perfect resonance with what you previously wanted.

The kind of thankfulness that is the key to bliss is the recognition of the quality, significance, and value of what you love about what is now. The pure energetic vibration of this breed of thankfulness which comes with attention that is given to the recognition of what you love about the present is the most receptive state of all—even more so than the state of stillness. It does not just allow Source to flow to you fully and uninterrupted—it also helps it flow to you. You are in perfect resonance with it.

Many people fear that if they appreciate what is, they will only get what is. This is not the case because your desire is inevitable, and as soon as you are in the space of thankfulness—regardless of what you are thankful about—what you desire will immediately manifest. You will get not only more of what you love in the present, but you will also no longer be introducing opposition to everything you want.

Thankfulness is the most beneficial state to be in. It is pure positive focus. It is unfiltered positive energetic vibration. You can start this practice first thing in the morning by being thankful for the day. You can mentally list things that you are thankful for upon waking. You can keep a gratitude journal in which you list all the things you are grateful for in the moment you are in and in your life right at the time that you pick up the journal to write. You may choose to keep an item with you, like a ring you wear that reminds you to find thankfulness for something anytime you see or feel it. There is no more beneficial thing to do in your physical life than to examine your world for things to be thankful about. They exist in every single situation there is. It is the moonlight in a jail cell. It is any thought, memory, scent, or kind word that kept you going. It is even in the role that has played negativity in your life. It is everywhere you look if you simply decide to look in the first place.

Focusing on the positive takes practice—like anything else that is new. It is good to have an arsenal of activities to do that train your awareness toward the positive. You can begin to consciously look for things that evoke a positive emotion within you. Ideally, this process will become habit for you no matter where you are or what you're doing. One good way to start this process is to start by taking a walk. The sole purpose of this walk is to look for things you like that feel good to you when you see, smell, or hear them. Instead of being just an observer who judges everything in your path on this walk, you will become like a hunter—a hunter of positives. Do not let your mind stray from the task at hand. If you come across something unpleasant, pay it no attention. Simply redirect your attention to scanning your surroundings and look for something pleasant. You can name the things in your mind as you come across them if it helps you to keep focused. It will surprise you, because you will most likely realize how dominant your negative orientation is now that you are taking control of it. It will also surprise you how fast this can change your mood.

By now, you have probably heard of the idea of an affirmation. An affirmation is a declaration of something positive that is currently true or that you want to be true. What you want to be true will become true, because physical truth is a feeling of validity that you have because something you have thought has now been thought regularly enough that it has manifested. You are sitting there, looking at the physical proof, which further reinforces your belief.

Some people think it is counterproductive to do affirmations because it can be confused as a form of lying to oneself. You can say, "I love myself," and upon saying that, feel bad because you don't currently love yourself. So it is easy to then say that the statement may be encouraging the feeling of not loving yourself instead of loving yourself. This is only true in the short term, because a belief is just a thought that has been repeated so much that the repetition has caused it to come to fruition.

The more a thought is repeated, the more it turns into a belief. So, the first thousand times you say the words "I love myself," you may not believe them—but eventually, with enough repetition, you will start to believe the affirmations you say. Once that happens, they will come to be. That being said, it is true that occasionally you may have practiced an energetic vibration or thought so long and believed it so fully that it was strong enough to introduce a contradictory energetic vibration which contradicted your sense of your own intelligence. Instead of attracting things that are an energetic vibrational match to the new, wanted energetic vibration or thought, you will attract only what is a match to your feeling of lack of intelligence. You will attract things that are a match to feeling wrong, and therefore you will attract evidence supporting your previous, unwanted energetic vibration. This will only make it more difficult to believe in the validity of the new thought. So, even more beneficial than repetition of things you don't yet believe in, is to approach affirmation in increments.

Instead of using an affirmation that makes you feel the full awareness of the current absence of what you want to be true, you can start first with an affirmation that already feels true. If you currently do not love yourself and saying you love yourself feels painful because it pulls you into awareness of the lack of love, you can use a bridge statement that does feel good, such as "I am excited for the day that I will wake up and feel love for myself." This is still an affirmation—and eventually, if you say it enough, affirming the statement "I love myself" will no longer carry with it the feeling of lack of love. It will instead carry love because it is not so far a jump to make from the place you are now to the place where that affirmation is true. It will feel good to you. The better your affirmations feel to you, the more effective they are.

You can have an affirmation journal in which you practice writing lists daily of any affirming statements that make you feel good. It would be even better, however, if you made them part of your running internal commentary. Whenever you notice yourself coming up with a derogatory comment to yourself or anything in your experience, you can counter it with a positive statement that actually makes you feel better in your mind. This practice is not meant to negate or stifle how you are feeling. If the statement you come up with feels like you are simply arguing with yourself and invalidating how you feel, it is not the right affirmation to use. The practice of affirmation is meant to teach you that you can shift the angles at which you perceive something. In doing so, you can maintain and create your own happiness.

Upon first embarking on the quest for positive resonance, many people do not yet realize that they have surrounded themselves with the essence of what they currently are instead of what they want to be. There is a very common saying in western society—"fake it till you make it." While this kind of pretending is degraded in society by being heralded as dishonesty, there is a vast element of universal truth in this saying. Everything that *is* was a thought first. Everything that *becomes* is a concept first. Everything you see starts as a trend toward the essence of that thing. This truth is easily demonstrated with the example of an Olympic gold medalist. Every Olympic dream starts as a poster on a child's wall first.

Olympic gold medalists do not spontaneously manifest the second they step on the podium, but they begin the minute they *desired* to stand on the podium. A gold medalist was for all the years they were training—for all the upsets as well as the achievements. The athlete was not faking being a gold medalist all the years they trained leading up to that moment. They were practicing the way they would act, feel, and look being an Olympic gold medalist, thereby becoming the essence, or energetic vibration, of being a gold medalist. Therefore, the athlete was an energetic vibrational match to being a gold medalist, and therefore they became one. It is only the idea that you are faking something instead of becoming the essence of it that turns this inherently positive idea into a negative one.

You can start the practice of becoming the essence of whatever you want—no matter where you are or what your life looks like—by realizing that the process of making it is a process. When a person looks at their life and says, "This is not what is, so I am faking it," it is that person who has condemned their own reality to the way it is. To the universe, there is no difference between pretend and real. There is only the energetic vibration of someone believing they are or believing they are not. Look at what surrounds you in the physical—your living space, friends, work, and hobbies. It is a very beneficial thing to then be objective and ask yourself honestly, "Is this healthy for me?" "Is this conducive to my bliss?" "Is this the way I want my life and my future to be?" and "Why?" It is greatly beneficial and can be very cleansing to then eliminate the immediate physical things that are not beneficial to how you want your life to be. However, removing things will not guarantee they will not come back again if your thoughts remain the same. Only the focus on what you want instead will do that.

A great exercise that will help you to use the Law of Attraction to your benefit is to spend time focusing on what you want and surround yourself with the essence of those things. It can be as simple as making a collage of things you cut out of magazines that you want to have, be, and do, as well as what you love. You can put it up somewhere in your space so you can focus on it daily. You can surround your home, office, car, or anywhere you spend time with the things that you want to be true for you. You can paint or draw what you want to be true, collect items that reflect what you want to be true, or surround yourself in colors that reflect what you want to be true. Display pictures of yourself and others that you want to be true, such as ones in which you and they are happy and healthy. Choose to spend time in locations that you want to be a part of. Find people who are already what you want to be.

Your life will become what you focus on. It will become the dominant energetic vibrations that you surround yourself with. Realize that you are the one who dictates whether you accept what *is* as the truth of your life or instead make true only what you want to be true for you. You do this by virtue of your undivided attention to it. You can now, knowing this, pre-write the story of your life. You can achieve this by doing an exercise in which you pretend you are the writer of a script or a novel—except you are writing about your own future. Pretend that whatever you write will come to fruition in your life—exactly to the last, minute detail. This will help you become very clear about your desires. It will also make it so you are holding yourself in the energetic vibration of your desires long enough so the signal you emit will be a bright beacon for the universe to answer quickly. Write an actual story in first person with yourself as the main character of how you want your life to be. You can write in conversation, if you like. The sky is the limit to this process. Nothing is too fantastical to eventually become a reality for you. You can use this to design your whole life or use it to design just a segment of your life. It is very helpful if you have an upcoming event that you are anxious about. Use it to help the event play out exactly as you want it to. You can pre-pave any number of future events with this pre-writing and pre-visioning exercise.

Another exercise that will help you immensely is to keep a journal of positives. In this journal, at the top of the page, you can write a subject (for example, "my job" or "today"), and then under the subject, write a page-long list of positive aspects of that subject. The subjects should be both things you love already and things you are feeling negative about. When you do this with subjects you are feeling positive about already, it will intensify that energetic vibration and make it even more dominant. When you do this with subjects you feel negative about, it deactivates the negative energetic vibration, starving it of energy. Listing your own positive aspects can be a very profound process.

You may, upon first glance, find within yourself a feeling of repulsion from the very idea of acknowledging your own positive aspects. In the culture we live in today, children are programmed against arrogance and bragging. Blatant acknowledgement of one's assets is shunned as if it is a sin. As a result, it has led to an unhealthy form of humility in which to get along in society. Indeed, to even be a good person—people are taught, and then believe that they must underrate or even berate themselves and their importance, strengths, and positive attributes.

There are many well-meaning (and many not-so-well-meaning) reasons for this, but the most important reason is that there has been a grave mix-up between ego and self-love. These two concepts are both misunderstood, and despite popular belief, they could not be more different if they tried.

Ego is a self-concept of identity that keeps us distinct. It is your idea or opinion of yourself in this life only. It is finite and separate, and it is what differentiates you from everyone and everything else you see as other. In truth, ego does not need to be a negative thing. Our self-concept is, after all, a part of what Source had in mind to have even created us in the first place. It is not a negative thing as long as it is not all we know of ourselves. Ego becomes negative when ego becomes either big or small—meaning that this separate identity is now defending its position, strengthening the illusion of separateness, and using comparison to be more than just different, but better than.

Ego, at its best, is a temporary point of view that helps the universe at large to evolve. Contrary to common understanding, ego becomes its worst self (big or small) not when someone loves themselves, but when a person is insecure. When a person becomes insecure, the ego goes in one of two directions—either in the direction of self-harming humility or in the direction of self-harming pride. Neither of these is healthy. Big ego, at its worst, is ignorance and self-harming pride. Small ego, at its worst, is ignorance and self-harming humility. On the side of self-harming humility, a person believes they are "less than." This person holds a punitive opinion of themselves and their importance in the world, such as their importance being underneath the rest of the world. The person has relinquished their incredibly important role and power in the universe at large and therefore is not living their full potential—and they are unhappy because of it. On the side of self-harming pride, a person is displaying arrogance and narcissism.

They are constantly in comparison to others in order to form an idea of themselves that is "better than." The person holds a grandiose opinion of themselves and their importance in the world in that they are above the rest of the world. This person has immense insecurity and therefore believes that in order to have worth, they must find a way to be more important than others. The person is not living their full potential, and is not happy because of it.

People suffering both conditions gravitate to each other, because they are a perfect energetic vibrational match to each other. This may sound strange at first, because they appear to be polar opposites. But they are identical, because the root they share is the energetic vibration of insecurity. Self-love is neither of these two extremes. Self-love is self-benefiting pride in a person who knows they are equal to others. A person who practices self-love has a healthy, loving, appreciative opinion of who they are and their incredible importance in the world. The person understands that everyone has strengths and weaknesses that are simply different instead of better or worse than anyone else's. They are able to recognize their strengths without having to wave them around as a means of gaining approval or power. The person is able to recognize their weaknesses without defeating their self-concept or having any effect on their self-worth. People practicing self-love are glad to be who they are. It is a state that is rooted in confidence instead of insecurity. A person who practices self-love has taken hold of their important role and power in the universe at large, is living their full potential, and is happy because of it.

People who love themselves do not harm others. They are in perfect energetic resonance with the opinion their higher self has of them. They feel the freedom and bliss of that attunement. It is a difficult practice to learn if self-love has been the baby thrown out with the bathwater of negative pride in your life. If we do not have self-love, we continually look for others to give it to us—but they cannot, because they are opposing energetic vibrations. We cannot harbor the absence of love for ourselves and attract anything other than others who do not really love us. We attract others who are just as insecure who are also looking to us to fill the void, and we can't do that for them, either. We also end up giving the only power we have away.

Your own self-concept is the one that dictates what opinions all others around you will have of you. There are many levels on which to start practicing self-appreciation. You can start with physical assets. Make a list of all of the physical assets you are appreciative of, such as, "I love my dark brown eyes," "I like my height," or "I look good when I wear blue." List anything you do actually like about your physical, three-dimensional self. The more you can come up with in any of these lists, the better. You can continue to add to them over months or even years.

Next, you can move on to personality assets. Make a list of all the things you appreciate about your personality, such as "I am warm," "I am open," "I am caring," or "I am dependable." If you're having trouble coming up with them on the spot, you can take out a dictionary or thesaurus and find words that express what you like about your personality.

Next, make a list of all the mental assets you have—things like "I am task-oriented," "I am good at math," or "I am confident about my ability to understand." After that, make a list of all the spiritual assets you have, such as, "I am intuitive," "I believe in life after death," or "I am spiritual." It can be anything you are proud of spiritually in yourself, regardless of anyone else's opinion of whether or not it is a good thing. What matters is that it is a good thing to you. Then write a list of your social assets—the things that make you a valuable member of society and valuable to others, such as "I am good at communicating," "I enjoy contributing," "I am a good listener," "I am a good example," or "I am well-organized." Then write a list of all the things you can think of that you have done in the past that you feel self-appreciation for doing. The list should be comprised of both achievements as well as displays of positive character traits. It can contain things like, "I established a close group of friends," "I graduated from college with a degree," "I lost five pounds," or "I stayed to take care of someone who was sick." Also, write a list of things you are currently doing and feeling that you are proud of, such as "I eat healthy most of the time," "I feel like I am capable," "I own my own home," or "I take good care of my children."

Lastly, write a list of what your favorite things about yourself are.

There can be repeats in this list that were in the previous lists. The point is that you are choosing to pick out and focus on what you supremely value in yourself. You are looking to recognize the good parts that you enjoy making a part of your healthy ego in this life. Go over these lists on days when you are feeling bad and when you are feeling good. You may find that these lists are very difficult to write. They may evoke a strong emotional reaction from you because upon writing them for the first time, you will suddenly have the comparison between what loving yourself looks and feels like and what the self-defeat you have been practicing for so long looks and feels like. You may feel sadness, guilt, or fear as a result of starting this shift of focus. That is okay, because it is just where you currently are—and you are changing where you are with this very exercise. You are ridding yourself of all the patterns of negative self-treatment you have harbored for so long, and movement of any kind can be painful at first when you are retraining your beliefs. The way you will feel and the way others will treat you will be an immediate improved reflection of this new orientation of focus toward yourself.

The practice of looking for what feels good can be something that you set up in advance in order to help you shift your energetic vibration to one of positivity when you are in a negative space. One of the best ways to do this is a spin on a technique that has been practiced in the field of psychology for years. You can create a large, covered container called a bliss box. When you are in a bad mood, the Law of Attraction is working to bring you to things that are match to that negative space. You will not gravitate toward positive things in a negative mental space. You will not even be able to notice them if they are in the room with you until you consciously change the thoughts you are thinking. You will want to create this bliss box when you feel very good, because when you feel very good, you are an energetic match to other things that further reinforce that good feeling.

Pick a container that in and of itself evokes a good feeling from you. In this bliss box, start to accumulate things that feel good to you—things that raise your energetic vibration. You can put a small collection of funny or inspiring movies in the container that you could put on to change your vibration, jokes, your favorite sayings, or a folder of pictures that make you feel joy. You can use photos that are both personal, such as photos of loved ones, and ones that are not, like things you've cut out of magazines or printed off the computer. You can put a small collection of music that makes you feel joy in the bliss box to play when you want to shift your mood. Put in small items that help you to feel joy in the chest, such as figurines, rocks, or a stuffed animal. You can put a book that uplifts you in the bliss box to pull out and read to improve your mood. Include a paint set or drawing set and paper to perhaps take out and start expressing yourself. You can keep a list of affirmations in this bliss box. Maybe you will even choose to keep your thankfulness journal, positive aspects journal, or positive self-assets lists in the bliss box to look over.

In this bliss box, you should also keep a list of as many things that you can think of that you know can raise your resonance—things you can't fit in the container itself, like taking a bath, massages, vacations, meditating, horseback riding, and dancing. Look over the list and pick something to deliberately get up, go find, or do. The sky is the limit with this bliss box. When you get into a negative emotional spot, if you can deliberately find the positive thought to go find this bliss box and then give yourself permission to rifle through it and utilize it to distract yourself and change your own vibration, the hard work will have already been done. Each positive thought you have will attract more and more positive thoughts, and you will find yourself feeling better. At this point any action you take will come from a positive emotional place instead of from a negative emotional space, and therefore, will be a positive action.

At this point in your life, there may be times when you find yourself trapped in a powerless, hopeless, fearful, or sad vibration. Train yourself to habitually practice a visualization that consciously brings your resonance higher into peace, readiness, and joy. Any visualization that best improves the way you feel is the perfect one to use. If you do not already have one that immediately comes to mind, you can try the following visualization.

To start, before you have this visualization memorized, you may wish to ask for someone to help by reading this to you out loud while you follow along and are guided by their voice. You could also record yourself and then play it while you are guided by your own voice.

To begin this visualization, find a comfortable space that you feel safe in. Allow your whole body to be supported. Inhale and exhale deeply a few times, filling your lungs to their full capacity and exhaling the air completely out of your lungs, making sure to exhale the residual air in the bottom of your lungs that is still present at the end of a normal exhalation. Then visualize breathing in comforting, warm energy that diffuses throughout your entire body. See it breaking up any negative energy there—any dark energy, tension, discomfort, or painful feelings. Visualize that negative energy being dislodged and released when you exhale. Feel it leave with your breath. Feel the in breath loosening, softening, and purifying your body.

Let your breath clean you of anything unwanted. Let go of it as the breath washes it from you, and replace it with a safe, easy sensation of relief. Now begin to imagine yourself in a place that makes you feel totally safe and peaceful. It can be a place you have been to once, a place you want to go, somewhere you have seen in a magazine, or a place that is totally imaginary and full of fantasy. It can be indoors or outdoors. As you lose yourself in the images and sensations of this place, let it become more real to you. Add as many details that make you happy. You can include items there that make you feel happy. You can include animals or a place to sit or lie down. You can add any sounds you love. Let yourself be swept up in the melody of the sounds. Feel the air on your skin and enjoy the sensation of it. It may be cold or hot, humid or dry.

Look to your right and left. Take in everything you see. Let the place completely surround you. Smell the scents of this place. It may be sharp, gentle, familiar, or made up. Maybe it's the smell of something baking in the oven. Maybe it's the salty scent of the ocean or the scent of someone you love. Know that you are the only person who has access to this place. It is there for you at any moment of the day. It is your private, impenetrable sanctuary of bliss.

As you realize this, feel yourself fill up with appreciation for this place. You feel Source in everything here. As you look to your feet, you realize that there is a healing energy here that can materialize. It is magic. You can see it there like a pool of glittering, white, liquid light. You dangle your feet into it. As you do, you can feel it. It is warm and tingling to the touch. You are enamored at its vibrancy. It is energizing, ethereal, and peaceful. It glows as if it is alive.

You notice that the liquid light is beginning to climb softly through your ankles and legs. It is intensifying and dancing, filling each body part that it touches with a gentle, blissful feeling of wonder. It surrounds each cell of your body—each vein and each bone. It protects and illuminates you as it climbs through your thighs, hips, and belly. Everything it shines through is fresh, full of beauty, and full of bliss. It is warm as it fills your abdomen and pours up through your chest, massaging each organ, relieving you of heaviness, and helping you release and open up to life. It nourishes your heart, dissipating any grief or sadness you hold there. It swirls around and through your spine. It diffuses into the marrow of your bones, where it becomes part of who you are. It radiates through your neck and throat, letting you know that everything you say has been heard and is being answered.

Your throat is now open for free expression. It spills up into your face and head, softening all the muscles in your face and filling the space behind your eyes, pouring in through your pupils to caress you and wash away any images you have seen in your life that made you feel negatively. Its vibrating softness weaves its way through your head and your thoughts, consuming any negative memories. You feel yourself letting go of them, letting the light take them from you. Let it wash away disappointments, grief, pain, or resentment. Let it pull all these things away from you. Let it awaken and enlighten you.

There is no barrier strong enough to resist the light. Like a fog being melted by sunlight, it all melts away in the brilliant warmth. It melts away to expose a pulsing, vibrating strength that is always within you. It is your purpose and your passion. You feel it in every fiber of your being. You remember your own vitality—your own eternal nature. It's as if you could almost touch it. It makes everything you have gone through in this life temporary.

You suddenly awaken again to how much more you are than just this life. You know with your whole heart and your whole being that you are free—that the heaviness you find yourself trapped in can be burnt away at any moment with your mind. You breathe in joy and light. It is what you are made of. You are healing. You understand your own vastness.

The light is throughout your entire body. It is radiating out into your ethereal body. It looks like a field of brilliant, angelic, prosperous, golden-white light emanating from you, touching everything around you with your own vitality—the infinity of your being. You know deeply that you can call forth this light and visit this place whenever you wish.

Spend however long of a time you want to spend taking it in, feeling the sensations of complete harmony—feeling divinity, joy, and experiencing total safety. Easily and gently—whenever you feel like it and with the knowledge that this light will be with you at all times—come mentally back into the room you are sitting in. Let your breath rhythmically come and go. Bring these feelings of deep harmony, healing, eternality, and joy with you into the room. They are yours to keep. When you feel ready, you can open your eyes. You are here.

A great tool that can also be used in the quest for positivity is a linear exercise that utilizes the contrast of your life to give birth to a positive resonance. If you can use a bit of willpower to remember to do it and then deliberately focus, it will become one of your favorite practices. It is a three-step process. When something happens that has put you in a negative emotional space, sit down and put a number one on a page. Next to it, write a small paragraph about what has happened and what you feel like right now as a result of it. Then below it, put a number two on the page. Next to that, write a paragraph about what that situation and feeling that way has caused you to know for sure that you want in your life. Below that, write a number three on the page, and next to that, write statements and affirmations that cause you to feel better about the situation you wrote about in number one—as many as you can think of—as well as anything you can think of to say that will bring you closer to feeling like the things you want (in number two) are a tangible reality for you. A good example could be:

1. I am very sick with the flu. I am not getting better very fast at all. It's making me feel hopeless, immune-compromised, and guilty, on top of feeling physically terrible, depressed, hopeless, overwhelmed, discouraged, doubtful, panicked, afraid, despaired, and powerless.

2. I want to be completely immune to anything I encounter. I want to be totally healthy, even if people around me are not. I want an amazing immune system. I want to walk through this world without fear of things I can't see. I want to feel physically good. I want to trust my body completely and know it has my best interest at heart.

3. A virus is just a manifestation of a vibration of collective negativity. If Source instantly becomes what I want, it can only ever be benevolent. If I am an extension of Source, I can only ever truly be benevolent, so I can trust that due to that, my essential self and my body only have my best interest at heart. I can let go and just let it take over and clear itself of the illness. I can trust my body. When I am throwing up, I am ridding myself of anything that doesn't serve me such as my old patterns, as well as the sickness itself. It is a good thing to get it out of me. It is only in my thriving that I can do anything for anyone. I do not need to resist the virus. Wholeness and health have already won a notable victory without fighting any battles simply by being what my Source, essential self already is. Because of that, now it is pulling me toward health like a magnet. My body will do exactly what it was designed to do. The human body is a marvel of technology. It's a machine of flesh and blood governed by the mind. Now is the time for me to be in relationship with my body and to treat it kindly for

what it is. How can I be in a kind and tender relationship with it? What could I eat that would allow it and me to feel cherished? What would expressing love to my body look like? These are the questions to ask, ponder, answer, and then enact. This too shall pass as everything is temporary. If I become convinced of my ability to be well, then I will get well very quickly. This is a great excuse to be lazy and watch movies.

In doing this exercise, you have put the negative experience in context to use it as a platform from which to design your life. You have gained great clarity as to what you want in life, and you will have released the energetic vibrations that introduce an opposition to what you want. This means that you will get what you desire quickly. The kind of thoughts you use in step three are the exact kind of thoughts that will become a habitual way of thinking and self-talk the more practiced you become in gaining control over your reality.

It is true that the pursuit of positive resonance is an individual journey—but it is also inevitable that other people will become participating components of this journey you are on. It has been well established so far that the underlying truth of this universe is one of unity. And so, you cannot ever help yourself without helping others.

The converse is also true. You cannot ever help others without helping yourself as well. It is for this reason that one of the best ways to achieve bliss is to give it to others. In other words, you can achieve bliss by engaging in random acts of kindness. Random acts of kindness are externally focused demonstrations of love. These acts can be both spontaneous and planned. They can come in many forms, such as the form of a gift, service, physical affection, positive words, or undivided time and attention. These random acts of kindness do not need to be elaborate. It can be as simple as letting someone merge in front of you on the highway, helping to wash the dishes, or just listening to someone who needs to be heard.

Aside from just taking opportunities as they are displayed to you, you can make a list of random acts of kindness so that if you are feeling negative, you can just pick one thing off the list to go do. It will lift your mood. As long as the random act of kindness does not come from a space of "I'm always the only one doing for others, and no one does for me," you will be initiating your own happiness by initiating it in another person. You will feel the immediate improvement of your mood as a result of it.

A great practice that you can begin today is to take some paper with you in the car when you drive somewhere and write a positive affirmative statement on the paper, such as "You are loved and appreciated every day" and let yourself be drawn to a specific parked car. The universe will draw you to the car that belongs to a person in need of that message. Anonymously place the note under the windshield wiper of that car. We are living in a society in which we are used to the only things placed on windshields being advertisements or traffic tickets. Imagine the happiness finding an unexpected note like that would bring to a person. And imagine if we all did that simple thing once every day—how good it would feel knowing you were the initiator of such happiness and change—not only in yourself, but also in the tone of the world.

CHAPTER 15
LET THESE HANDS BE YOUR
HANDS: HOW TO CONTRIBUTE
TO OTHER PEOPLE'S BLISS

Your name like dusk
And mine, like dawn.
One, the end of a new beginning-
the other, the beginning of a certain end.
In between, the light of day affords a glimpse of an axiom,
unseen through the covered lens of our separate sight.
That there has not been a moment
where our beginning and end has not been one and the same.
So let these hands of mine be your hands.
They have been orphaned as you have been orphaned.
They have bled as you have bled,
They have ripened in the sunshine of your joy.
So let them give back now that which they have taken.
Let all that remains of them be yours from this day evermore.

We come into this physical dimension deliberately with the intention of experiencing our separate realities in conjunction. This was our intention so we could use one another as catalysts to our own evolution. The evolution of all that is, is the result of our interactions with each other, whether they are positive or negative in nature.

We experience life from an individual perspective. Because of this, we have often felt cut off from everything that we perceive as being outside of that individual perspective. In that illusion of being cut off, the concept of self-reliance and independence has become quite a celebrated trait that is imposed on each generation—but physical self-reliance is a complete illusion. A person may say, "I am independent in the fact that I do not need anyone's help to get food. In fact, when I am hungry, I simply drive to the store and get some." However, in this scenario, the realization of this person's food was dependent on the existence of the car. This is therefore every element going into the construction of that car, the gas running the car, the roads the car drives on, the existence of the store, the farmer who grew the food, the shipping of the food, the people who prepared the food, the currency with which to buy the food, and much more. The realization of food in this scenario, which was interpreted as an independent act, was in fact dependent on many things outside that individual person.

Every aspect of your physical life comes as a result of your own focus and your own connection with your higher self and Source, so your abundance is never at the mercy of others—but it almost always comes to you via the route of others. All you see with your eyes outside of yourself is a manifestation of Source. Because your existence is dependent on Source, you are therefore living in an interdependent universe with all that you see. We should not look outside ourselves for happiness, because the key to it is within our individual selves. Paradoxically, much of our happiness comes to us in the physical form of others. We yearn for intimacy and connection from others. In this connection, we feel love for another, and when a person becomes enlightened to the full truth of oneness that exists as the foundation of even our separate physical forms, that love of another turns into love of all that is other. It is obvious that we would inevitably reach a place where we would want to participate in the creation of happiness in the lives of others as well as in our own lives.

First, it is important to understand that you are helping them with your very existence. Regardless of the role you play, you cannot escape the fact that you are a part of the creation of everyone else's reality. If a person is playing a negative role in another person's life, that person exists as a three-dimensional comparison for the person to better understand what they dislike and therefore identifies and creates what positive thing they would like to be, have, or do instead. The inevitable result of this process is evolution. In fact, the catalysts for the greatest things in our lives are often the people we identify as the worst people in our lives. When a person is playing a positive role in another person's life, they are serving as a three-dimensional example that helps the other person to identify and therefore create the positive thing they want to be, do, or have. Though you cannot escape this perpetual beneficial role you play in other people's lives, it is up to you whether you play the role of negative comparison or positive example.

All matter in this universe at its root potential energy contains at once two paradoxical aspects—the existence of the thing and the nonexistence of that same thing. Just as darkness is the absence of light, negativity is the absence of positivity. You can, at any point, focus upon either paradoxical aspect and attract the exact essence of that into your life. For example, you could focus upon someone's perfect health and what that looks like, even if it is not a current reality- or you could focus on the absence of someone's physical health and what that looks like.

A person's life also contains these two aspects. They come in the form of what it is that they desire and the absence of what it is that they desire. As with everything else, a person has a choice of which of these aspects they focus on, which therefore determines the reality before them. You also have a choice of which aspect of this person's life you are going to focus on and therefore help them become. What a person is being currently is only part of the picture of the totality of that person. You can choose to focus on, and therefore add to the vibration of the negativity another person practices now—the absence of where they want to be. You can focus on the absence of where you want them to be, the absence of their joy, the absence of their health, the absence of their success, and how they act now as a result of that absence. Or you can choose to focus on what is already a part of that person's current state that is positive—where that person wants to be, where you would wish them to be, what joy looks like for them, what health looks like for them, what their success looks like, and how they would act if they had the presence of everything they desire.

One of the best things you can do for other people is to stop focusing on the negative, which is the absence of positive things in the person's life, and turn focus to the positive, which is the presence of positive things in the person's life, with regards to that person. Shower other people with what you love about them and what they are capable of. You can reflect back to them their own goodness, strength, and love. When you do this, you are showing them the reflection of their true natures. You will mirror their solution instead of their problems. You are making what you focus on part of your own desire, and what your higher self has already energetically become the second you desire it. As such, due to the Law of Attraction, the universe will pull these people toward those things as if magnetically. You will be helping to create these things for them.

You cannot focus upon the absence of positive things in other people's lives and feel good. This is because focus upon the absence of the positive in someone else is not a point of view that your higher self agrees with. You cannot resonate with your higher self when you are doing so. And when you don't achieve resonance with your higher self, you will experience negative emotion. However, if you are in a space of positive emotion and are in total resonance with your higher self, the laws of this universe dictate that you cannot be matched with negativity. This means that you can only ever find resonance with, and therefore be an energetic match to, people's positive attributes and desires. If you are an energetic match to their positive attributes and desires, you can help people. If you cannot find resonance with their positive attributes and desires, you cannot help them. You will simply strengthen the energetic vibration of negativity, or the absence of the positive aspects of their life. Whereas from the space of bliss, which is total resonance with Source, you cannot be a match to their negativity because you will only ever be matched with their positivity. This means people who will not resonate with your positive energetic vibration will simply, and with ease, drift out of your experience.

You will only be able to share your reality with someone of whom you are an energetic vibrational match to—either to this person's current positive space or positive desires—so you can both enjoy and help them. It is for this reason that the single most important thing you can do for another person is to find bliss, or resonation with your higher self and Source for yourself. If you have not been self-centered enough to have done this, you will have nothing to give to others anyway. When you have been self-centered enough to have done this, everything else will simply fall into line. The Law of Attraction will orchestrate all of it. You will only be brought to those you can help. You may do it without even realizing you are doing it. It will not feel like effort to do so, but it will instead fill you with joy to do so. It will feel good enough that it will not feel like a favor. You will not even feel as though it was something you did for another person, but instead, you will feel as though it was something you did for yourself. You will never need gratitude from another person to make it feel good. You will only ever be an energetic vibrational match to the solution, and never again to the problem.

It would, in fact, be accurate to say that the best way to help others is to realize that you cannot help others. You cannot impose anything on anyone—help included. A person is only ever able to be helped when they are able to receive help. A person can only receive help when they are receptive and therefore willing to focus on their desires instead of the absence of them. All you can really do is find your own bliss, and from that state, where you are only a match to other's desires, those who are in the receptive state can use you to help themselves. The universal truth is that this is the only type of help there is or ever was.

If you are a person who has set up your idea of goodness around the type of help that involves effort and sacrifice, this truth may feel like a bit of a letdown. It may sound selfish, *but* this physical dimension was meant to be experienced from our own personal point of view. Nothing—including help—can ever be imposed, and the true nature of this universe is one of eternal oneness. The best way to help, heal and bring happiness to others, is by helping, healing and making happy the epicenter of all that is, which is yourself. Your mission on earth is not to fix others or change what is outside yourself. This universe is not one of finite size, but it is infinite. This means you cannot get poor enough to make someone else rich, and you cannot suffer enough to make someone else happy. Your job is to shift what is inside of you and from there, watch others and the external world change and become more as a result of that. If you are in a space of resonance with your higher self, you may very likely be compelled to help when the opportunity presents itself—but it was never your job to help others.

We are all in this existence because of Source's continual attention to our existence. We cannot *be* physically if Source withdraws its consciousness from us. There is not one single unit of this physical dimension—living or non-living—that is alone or forsaken. No matter how low someone's state is perceived to be, they always have this constant connection to Source, whether they are in the practice of allowing or opposing it. Source pulls everyone toward their desires—and everyone's desires toward them—with no exception. It does not matter if a person opposes this pull and ignores their emotional compass all of their life—it will never cease to be. It will never cease to be, because a person's connection to Source will never cease to be. A person will experience the realization of their desires the minute they allow them in. The realization of abundance is constant, whether it is in the form of a person manifesting a million-dollar mansion or a half-eaten sandwich in a garbage can on the side of the street.

We run into trouble with others by imposing our point of view on top of others' points of view about their own lives. When most people see someone homeless in the streets, it creates strong negative emotion such as sadness in them. This negative feeling is not actually because of the discordant relationship between the state the homeless person is in and the state the homeless person wants to be in. It is because of the discordant relationship between the state the homeless person is in and the state we want the homeless person to be in. Our sadness for homeless people is not an indicator of what they desire, but it is an indicator of what we desire. To really help someone achieve bliss means to help them to find resonance with what they want for their lives. When you make what they want something that you want for them, the Law of Attraction is now working twice as hard toward it.

It is perfectly fine to desire something for someone else that they do not yet desire for their own. But this is still your own desire for that person. It is the overlaying of our personal opinion that makes us feel sorry for another. We could use the sight of another person suffering as comparison to help us identify what we want for others. The best thing to do would be to find resonance with that desire for that person, and from that space, be inspired toward some action that is a match to our own desire. Too often, though, instead of using it as the basis for improvement, we continue complete focus on the suffering. We use it to justify our false beliefs of victimhood about the world. We cannot see what a person could possibly be getting out of their own negative situation. We cannot believe that anyone would choose to be birthed into negativity. We do not understand that people create their lives once they are here in the physical—whether it is on purpose or by default. We cannot see that their ideas of what is possible for them are not the same as our ideas of what is possible for them—and so the discord about their current situation is much greater in us than it is in them. We form the idea then that this life is unfair and that things can happen at random in a cosmic crap shoot.

While it is easy to come to these conclusions if we are in a space of not understanding the purpose of life or our own role in it, they are universally untrue. We cannot achieve resonance with our higher selves, or bliss, from the standpoint of these false concepts. There is no help you could ever give someone from your separate physical state that would ever come close to the magnitude of the help Source gives to them. When you are inspired to help, you are just a collaborative element of Source's help. It is best to find a way to trust others in this unbreakable connection. You can help others by giving them the invaluable gift of understanding.

Understanding helps others to release opposition to where they are. It helps them feel strong enough to pull focus away from where they are and turn in the direction of where they want to be. It is also an invaluable trait to learn with regards to other people, because it helps us release opposition to where they are and what they are thinking. From that platform of understanding, we can turn in the direction of what we want for them. We can also learn to trust. If we are to find resonance with our higher selves and bliss, we must trust others to find their own ways. We must trust others to manifest their own help. If you are, in fact, the help they have manifested, helping will feel good and easy instead of overwhelming.

Trust that others have their answers even if they don't think they do, and that the answers will come to them. Trust that people can realize their wants and bliss from whatever space they are in mentally or physically. Some people are in a place of such opposition to their higher selves that they hit rock bottom before they recreate their own life, and some die. Though unnecessary, neither way is wrong. Trust that no one is ever abandoned by Source. Everyone is being constantly pulled toward their own wants and their own bliss. It is never your responsibility to help another—but it may very well be your capability.

Over the centuries, there have been many arguments between cultures and teachers promoting bliss through the concept of selflessness and those promoting bliss through the concept of self-centeredness. As a result of the focus on the conflict between these seemingly opposing philosophies, we have been blind to the thread of truth that runs through both of these philosophies. The self-centeredness supported by self-focused teachers does not conflict with the externally oriented kindness supported by pro-selflessness teachers. These two philosophical viewpoints appear to directly oppose each other only because of language and the fact that both viewpoints are different angles to look at the same truth. In society, the term selfishness generally refers to greedy, uncompassionate, or narcissistic motivations, which are not viewpoints in line with Source. As such, these viewpoints create discord in the person being selfish and therefore bring about suffering. In contrast, self-focus refers to acting out of one's own interests, including indirect interests, which is in line with Source. You cannot act out of interest for yourself and not by default be acting out of interest for all that is other.

All people are inherently self-focused because a person experiences, desires, and forms values based on their own individual perspective. A person then makes their decisions in an attempt to best fulfill those desires and values. Everything that is ever done or ever has been done is done because the person doing it is convinced that they will feel better by doing it. What is in the best interest of oneself is never narcissism, greed, or lack of compassion, because these traits are the result of painful discord with Source. While everyone is self-interested—and this is how physical life was intended to be experienced—the label "selfish" is not the same thing as the self-centeredness that these cultures and teachers promote.

Generally speaking, what most pro-selflessness cultures and teachers call selflessness could very well be called kindness or compassion. Using the term "selflessness" suggests that a selfless person does not experience life from their individual perspective, does not have any desires or values, and that the person does not act out of their perspective or desires at all. This is impossible. It would defy the entire reason for physical existence. But that is not what most pro-selflessness cultures and teachers mean. When they call a person selfless, what they mean is that the person has a compassionate perspective, desires, and values that compel them to focus on the bliss of other people. A selfless person by this definition has discovered that other people's happiness attracts their own happiness. In acknowledgement of oneness, there is no way to make other people unhappy and achieve happiness yourself, just as by lending to other people's bliss, you are lending to your own.

In contrast to the misnomer, the philosophy of selfless bliss refers to people who have kind and compassionate interests that they act out, as opposed to not having interests or not acting out of their interests. Selfishness and selflessness can be completely compatible philosophies, because the former can mean self-focus and the latter can mean kindness—both of which are integral to bliss. Self-interestedness is completely compatible with kindness. We feel good when we observe others feeling good. We feel bad when we observe others feeling bad. We feel enjoyment and satisfaction by helping other people and by making other people feel happy. You can be most helpful to others by always being in resonance with your higher self by finding bliss yourself, because the true nature of this universe is one of eternal oneness.

The topic of others within our reality brings up the rather complicated subject we call love. Many cultures have multiple words for all the different kinds of love there are. In the English language—the language in which this information is first being offered—the word love can refer to such a plethora of experiences it is almost dizzying. It can be the word used to represent feeling states, attitudes, pleasures, or strong affections felt for any number of things from romantic attachments to sexual attachments to platonic attachments. This practice of using one term to cover a wide variety of definitions as well as complex emotional states is partly responsible for the confusion most people alive today have with regards to the idea of love. It is perhaps, then, a beneficial thing to introduce you to the way the universe at large sees love. Yet again, it is a feeling space rather than a cerebral concept. It is an experience rather than an intellectualization, and so using words to explain it is difficult.

To Source, or your transcendental and eternal self, love is not just an emotion or a virtue. It is the basis for all physical and non-physical being. All things created were created from love to love. It is the profound- feeling space of total and complete oneness. Because Source is constantly in the reality of oneness, it is in the state of constant, unconditional love. Because we are in the space in this three-dimensional reality of separateness, unconditional love is a feeling space. It is a mental attitude- a decision we make, and most importantly, a skill to be developed. Love is not something that either exists or does not exist in us toward ourselves and others. Loving is something we learn to do.

Loving unconditionally is a lifelong practice. Loving unconditionally is not something that can be experienced outside of the parameters of worth. If you are still basing the worth of yourself or others on externals such as what a person does and says, or another person's talents, someone's gender, a person's aptitudes, or someone's shortcomings- then you are practicing conditional love. To unconditionally love is to see the true essence of your own worth as well as the worth of others. To unconditionally love others is to see that worth has nothing to do with externals or anything they will leave behind upon leaving this life. To see the identical nature of everyone's core essence is to allow yourself, in that recognition, to experience the unchanging, eternal-feeling space of that unity regardless of any conditions that differentiate you from them in this life. In truth, you could say that love is a kind of spiritual awareness.

No one on this earth deliberately practices conditional love. But most people practice conditional love by default. They do not know any other way to love—not only because it is the kind of love that is demonstrated to them (and people learn primarily by example), but also because most people have forgotten their eternal, non-physical, true nature. When you feel bad due to focus on something you dislike about yourself or someone else, you are using that thing as your excuse to disallow Source and therefore love to come into your life as it naturally would without the prevention of it. You are, in that moment, saying that your love is conditioned upon that external thing changing before you can feel love—which couldn't be further from the truth. Nowhere is this more paramount than in your relationship with yourself. No suffering is ever about another person. It is always the result of the relationship with yourself. You can never get anything else other than external relationships that are in exact energetic vibrational resonance with the internal relationship you have with yourself.

The real question to ask yourself is, "Am I practicing unconditional love with myself?" If you do not feel unconditional love for yourself, it feels terrible, because it is an opinion toward yourself that your higher self does not share. You will feel the disharmony of that extreme lack of resonance with yourself. The person with whom unconditional love must start is with the epicenter of all that is in your reality—yourself. From there, the unconditional nature of your love will reflect out across everything else in your life. No achievement could ever fill the void where self-love should be. No one else could ever love someone enough to compensate for their own lack of self-love. To get love, you must give it. You cannot give it if you do not give it to yourself.

It may seem a bit backward that the second you are able to get love from someone else is the second you do not need it because you have already achieved it within yourself and no longer experience the need for it. But this is how the universe works. In truth, you cannot gain anything from the need of it. This is because need is the energetic equivalent of "not having," and so the only thing that is an energetic vibrational match to that thing is more "not having." It is only when you get to the energetic vibrational space by training your thoughts to already vibrate whatever it is that you want, that you can actually tangibly get what you want. The real way to get unconditional love is to ask yourself what unconditional love of yourself would look and feel like to you and then focus solely upon that in your life. Choose to give your attention to what you do like about yourself. Try to reach for the feeling space of your true, essential nature. Don't condemn yourself for any externals you have picked up in your physical life, including the fact that you may be experiencing the lack of love for yourself at this instantaneous, temporary point in time.

It may take a good amount of time to gradually train yourself into self-love, as it undoubtedly took some time for you to be influenced out of self-love. It does not matter how long it takes. All that matters is that you are withdrawing your focus from anything that feels bad to think about yourself and refocusing on things that feel good to think about yourself.

This simplistic practice may seem no match for the daunting task of really loving yourself unconditionally, because it could have been something that has eluded you for years. The fact of the matter is that self-love usually eludes people for years because they overcomplicate it and do not realize it is within their power at any moment to think thoughts different from those that are not deliberate and therefore immediate. Behaviors and actions that are an energetic match to those thoughts will then follow directly and effortlessly. Practicing kind thoughts that are an energetic match to self-love will help you experience your worth in all its full bounty, because genuine kindness is the three-dimensional manifestation of love. Once you begin to manifest it toward yourself, it can do no other than manifest toward everyone else in your experience.

CHAPTER 16
YOUR TRUTH, YOUR LIFE

You cannot have a life,
You cannot lose a life,
You are life.
Let your tears be no more than
the glittering aftermath of revolution.
For your smile is the doorway to bliss, blown open by the proud
Cathedral of your laughter whose bells
can be heard ringing on eternally
even in the steadiness of breath.
Lay down your fear and come to know the gospel of your glory
And Make yourself ready to become anything
You should ever want to become.

We are in a time of great change. This time, which has been called the time of reawakening or the new age, is a time in which conformity will cease to be a possibility. We are reawakening beyond these temporary, individual cycles from one birth to one death into the truth of oneness and our divine purpose. The format of our schools, justice systems, governments, and societies will be unsupportable as they now are. They will change, because the purpose of our physical life is evolution.

Evolution cannot come of one idea or one set of standards that all people agree upon and meet. We do not want it, either. The illusion of that desire comes only from insecurity. Flexibility is the order of the day. The conformity that is the goal and platform of today's society is a completely different concept from the unity that is universal truth. In fact, it is in direct defiance of it.

There are children being born who are coming into this life with the intention of being not only unwilling, but also unable to change certain aspects of themselves. This inability to change in order to conform is a decision they make prior to living their physical lives. It is a decision that will force the rest of physical society into deciding to change. They are coming into this life as a result of the oppression and rigidness felt by previous generations as well as those of us alive today. In that oppression and demand for conformity, we have formed the strong desire for change within society. This type of contagious and collective asking is, in fact, the very cause of species evolution that has been going on for billions of years on this planet. These new children are coming as the beginning of the answer to our asking. They are catalysts. People will look for one scientific reason behind this great wave of children who deviate from what is standard.

As with any variation from what is normal, people will argue about the root cause. They will identify physical precursors. But the sheer numbers being born with no external explanation that can be agreed upon and solved will eventually force society to look beyond the physical vantage point. The format of our institutions will no longer serve the majority so they will change out of necessity. Human beings' relationships with one another across all cultures are changing. From where we are now, it is possible that our conflicts will provide so much suffering that the way we were going about it, such as each group of people in a struggle for power, will no longer make sense and will be abandoned for the understanding that no matter what color, creed, religion, or culture- we are all one.

We, as humans are slowly turning into a new species. The earth itself is in transition as well. As is always the case with change, it is a personal choice how one responds to these changes. Those who resist the change will suffer, and those who allow it will experience great freedom. It does not need to be something we fear. We can experience great joy through this change the more we learn to allow each other. Allowing each other is not the same as forcing ourselves to like what we do not like and accept that it is how it is. To allow is to stop thinking our happiness depends on them changing. To allow is to stop trying to force them to change. It is relaxing that everyone has had different experiences, and those different experiences mean that they have different desires and different points of view. You needn't fear those differing desires or points of view affecting you at all. You can only experience what you make yourself an energetic vibrational match to. You can have, do, or be anything that you want- regardless of other people agreeing or disagreeing with you. If you allow other people, it is not only the grounds for helping others to be happy, but also the grounds to release your opposition to what you truly want, so that in the absence of the opposing thoughts, it may manifest in your life. Allowing others to *be* is essential to making other people happy. It is essential to your happiness to find a way to allow others who are not allowing you.

You have a choice when you meet with any kind of negativity, be it fear, sadness, anger, or pain. The choice is to take one of two paths. The first path is to let it be a catalyst to closing yourself off. When you take this path, you decide to use pain as the tool to sharpen yourself and make yourself harder in the attempt to keep suffering out. The second path is to let negativity be a catalyst to open yourself up. When you reach the level of wisdom that enables you to choose the second path, you will see that it is possible to live twenty-four hours a day in a state of joy. Every thought you create, movement you make, and word you speak can be infused with love, because love and joy are one and the same. Let love and joy grow in you, and one day, you will embrace the whole of the world in compassion and understanding. The suffering in this world will diminish. There will be an end to anger, sadness, neglect, violence, addiction, war, and fear. All of the barriers we build between each other will dissolve. You will know this truth, because you had it all along. But this brings up the very dichotomy of truth itself.

Truth is defined by many as something proven to be actuality, reality, or fact. This presents a problem, because you create your reality. Your reality is only a manifestation of what others have previously thought, which you have agreed with as well as what you have previously thought and through your thought attracted into your experience. All you have actualized cannot exist separate from you. It is also never static, so it cannot be fact. Proof can never exist separate from the expectation of the person who is searching for it.

One might ask why one should speak of truth at all. It is because there are two kinds of truth. The first is subjective truth. The second is objective truth. Subjective truth is the rational actuality that you have come to from your separate physical life. It is limiting, dependent on the brain and logic, and fits into the parameters of the tool of language. It is completely individual. Subjective truths are things like "there is a heaven," "I am a man," or "Junk food will make me fat." You create your own subjective truth. You are living your own subjective truth.

Objective truth, on the other hand, which many call absolute truth, is a truth that exists separate from the brain. It is unattached to finite things like the self. The word truth is derived from the old English, Norse, and

German words that mean fidelity, loyalty, sincerity, veracity, and perhaps most importantly, faith, and belief. These elements to the word *truth* apply directly to objective truth, because objective truth is ineffable. It can truly only be felt. While objective truth can be filtered into its closest language resemblance, objective truth is the feeling space behind a subjective truth. It involves faith. It exists inside every single person, and it is no different from person to person. It is an internal, essential knowledge. One has access to internal knowledge through their emotions. Emotions are not only keeping you in touch with your wants but also with objective truth. Objective truth is universal truth. It is the same for everyone, but you find access to it individually. No one else can do it for you. Your connection to it is never broken. It can, however, be resisted or allowed. Objective truth is never realized externally, and eternal subjective truth may only serve as a catalyst to the realization of it. It is for this reason that you should never be threatened by what anyone else considers to be true. It cannot impose itself on you.

You can choose whether to assume subjective truth based on whether or not it feels like an energetic match to the objective truth within you. You cannot lose your objective truth. You cannot get objective truth wrong. You can only ever decide to assume subjective truths that contradict it. Trust that you have this. Trust that others also have this. No matter what state you are in now, objective truth is pulling you toward itself, as if magnetically. No matter what state someone else is in now, objective truth is pulling that person toward it as well. You are living your life according to your subjective truths and their relation to objective truth, from the stand point of your separate, physical self.

Everything about the subjective truth of your separate physical life is a choice. You have the choice to live your subjective truth according to objective truth. The choice always was, always is, and always will be yours. You will know, the closer you get to objective truth, that the human eye deceives you. Nothing here is motionless. We have temporarily- from the clay of Source- been thrown into and out of form. We walk through this world of our own creation. It is a projected expression of the very same medium that makes up all that is.

Only one medium exists in this universe, and that is the medium of Source. Therefore, the only hand you can ever shake is your own. The only street you can walk on is yours. The only thing you can ever love is yourself. You meet yourself in everything you see. Your life is a liberated existence the second that you know it is. Your joy, will, and wants can never be separate from those of Source, because you are Source, and Source is you. There is no sculptor in the sky designing your life for you, because the sculptor in the sky is you.

GLOSSARY

Akashic: Of or pertaining to Akashic record, the Akashic record is the totality of information about all that ever was and is, which is encoded in the non-physical plane of existence, also referred to as the mind of God. It is a collection of unlimited information which can be accessed from the state of Source like consciousness such as when one is in meditation, while astral planning or under hypnosis. Accessing the Akashic record allows for omniscience.

Ascension: A rise of consciousness in an individual or totality. During ascension, the energetic vibration of an individual or totality will rise in amplitude and frequency.

Angel: Angels are also a type of guide. Often they are the least manifested and therefore the most vibrationally resonant with Source itself. Though they do not often project themselves with the image of wings, the traditional image of a person with wings, is an image they have chosen which has helped people identify with what they are and their purpose. They use the imagery of wings because wings have long been a symbol for humans of the "messenger." It was even more so the symbol of a spiritual messenger when Judea Christianity came about and so, it was a symbolic image that resonated very strongly with the people who were alive at that time. Because of the overwhelming Christian influence that still exists today, this is still a symbolic image that speaks to people of their purpose. And so, they can and do still appear in this way, if it is the format that will best be received by whomever they are relating with.

Astral plane: A non-physical plane of existence parallel to the physical reality. Though Source does not experience existence from the standpoint of a "place" or a "level," for the sake of physical understanding, astral plane is the place of Source. To "astral plane" is the act of consciously or subconsciously shifting consciousness from the perception of physical to the perception of non-physical which is unlimited by distance and time therefore a person who has the ability to astral plane, can visit any point in space or time instantly and even gain information from the fore mentioned experience.

Aura: The thought form both transmitting and receiving information to and from the body. To some, it is perceived through the senses. An aura often exhibits shapes, colors, textures, hues, sounds, patterns and emanates light. It is thought to have an electromagnetic nature. Differences in aura colors are perceived because the distribution of light particles versus the wavelength in any given electromagnetic field varies greatly (due to differing energetic vibration). Any or all of these characteristics of an aura can tell a practitioner of energy valuable information about the physical person or thing the aura is associated with. They can tell a nearly complete story of who you are. An aura will respond to a thought and change its characteristics to match that thought.

Chakras: The "force centers" of energy within and of the physical body. They could be considered the focal points for the reception and transmission of energies to and from the physical body.

Channel: The process in which a person gives either conscious or subconscious permission for another thought form to meld with their perceptual and cognitive capacities with the intent of transmitting information.

Clairvoyance: The apparent power to perceive things which are not present to the normal and physical senses, but which manifests it's self most dominantly through the "mind's eye." Clairvoyants often receive extrasensory information in the form of visualizations. It is sometimes called "inner sight." Foretelling the future is a form of clairvoyance.

Clairsentience: The apparent power to perceive things which are not present to the normal physical senses but which manifests it's self most dominantly through the ability to acquire extrasensory knowledge by means of feeling. A clairsentient person is able to perceive energy fields through physical sensations.

Clairaudience: The apparent power to perceive things which are not present to the normal physical senses but which manifests it's self most dominantly through the ability to perceive auditory stimuli which is beyond the normal range of hearing, regardless of distance or time. It is the supernormal hearing of sounds or verbalizations. Clairaudience includes the ability to receive audible perceptions of ghosts, spirits or that which exists in the astral realm.

Consciousness: United, objective awareness. It is the state of "God" or "Source". It is a state with a transcendent quality. Though there are many levels of consciousness, the manner in which it is used here means the aware state of God, which is empty of self, empty of judgment and empty of identity.

Dimension: The minimum number of coordinates needed to specify each point of a space or object. For example, a line has a dimension of one because only one coordinate is needed to specify a point on that line. It also refers to the basic structure of space and its position in time. We live in a universe of multiple dimensions.

Divine: A quality or emanation of Source.

Empath: The apparent ability to perceive things which are not present to the normal physical senses but which manifests it's self most dominantly through the ability to psychically read and assume the emotions or realities of others. It is a "feeling" type of extrasensory ability except instead of information being received in the form of physical sensation it is received through the emotional channel.

Energetic Vibration: The amplitude and frequency of energy, which is what determines how, or in what form that energy will express itself. Everything in the universe vibrates, and everything that vibrates imparts or impacts information. This "vibration" is what determines in what form energy will manifest. Only information which has expressed it's self at or slower than the speed of light, is received by our physical senses, in a three dimensional reality. Information present within energy in its potential state expresses its self-based on thought or intention.

Energy: An innate, universal force flowing within and between all things, making up all that is. It both manifests and de manifests, exhibiting a dynamic quality which is of useable power. It exists in many forms such as kinetic energy, mechanic energy, or potential energy. It is in a state of Potential and contains at once all possible information and all possible outcomes until it is activated into one state or another.

Enlightenment: The opening up to ultimate clarity of perception, understanding, awareness and knowledge, a state of complete allowance to the energetic vibration of Source. Enlightenment is in fact not an achievement; it is a moment to moment practice, though traditionally, to cultures which believe in karma, enlightenment has been seen as an achievement which ends the soul's cycle of death and birth.

Esoteric: Things pertaining to the non-physical reality, thus pertaining to inward focus which makes them take on a certain kind of "mystical" quality. The dictionary often defines esoteric also as information which is meant for and understood by a chosen few, by those specially initiated, or of rare or unusual interest. It is incredibly inaccurate to say that esoteric information is meant for the few. Esoteric information simply does not tend to be the focus of the majority of people throughout human history so traditionally it is only consciously understood by a minority of individuals. Esoteric information is something which is inherent within all things, but must be awakened to.

Eternity: An infinite existence outside the parameters of time and space.

Extrasensory: That which is traditionally thought to be beyond or outside the normal range of the physical senses of sight, smell, taste, feel, sound, emotion. Extrasensory perception is the ability to perceive that which is outside the range of the ordinary senses.

Higher Self: The portion of Source within and of the physical body, which remains non-physical and therefore maintains the energetic vibration of Source regardless of what energetic vibration, is held in the physical. When one accesses and assumes the point of view of the higher self, they can live in a state of enlightenment.

Inner Peace: A state of being mentally and spiritually tranquil, harmonious and free.

Intuition: Immediate cognition of knowledge and belief that is obtained without the use of reason, logic or ration. That does not need justification to remain true. Intuition is also often called a "hunch" or "instinct".

Karma: The concept that an action or deed can be the causal origin of a cycle of cause and effect which is now fated. It is often referred to in eastern culture as "Samsara." By most who believe in Karma, it is thought that humans have free will to choose good or evil and suffer the consequences, which are then in forced by the greater energy of "The Immense Ultimate," or "God." By believers, the karmic effects of all deeds are viewed as actively shaping past, present, and future experiences. It applies on all levels from day to day all the way to multiple lifetimes.

Law Of Attraction: A universal principal of a fundamental interaction within the universe. The principal of "that which is like unto it's self is drawn". The Law of Attraction is the "director force" of all energetic vibrations within the universe. It is directing energetic vibrations that resonate together and energetic vibrations that are not a resonating match away from each other on the level of spirit, on the level of thought and on the level of physical alike. The Law of Attraction argues that thoughts (both conscious and unconscious) can affect things outside the head, not just through motivation, but by other means as well. Observance of the Law of Attraction is the origin of the thought behind karma.

Meditation: An altered state of consciousness in which a person allows themselves to go beyond the physical and mental state to resonate with the energetic vibration of Source and therefore enlightenment. It is a state of being absent of cognitive thought.

Medium: A person possessing extrasensory abilities who someone who is able to serve as an intermediary, or translator between that which is physical and that which is non-physical in nature. Mediums are best known for facilitation communication between the living and non-living.

Meridians: Energy focused into channels which gives rise to the exactness of the physical structure we experience as the body. From a physical standpoint, they are often seen as being within the body. But they are in fact the patterning of energy creating the network of our complex physical bodily patterns.

Monism: A metaphysical philosophy that heralds all of non-physical and physical reality, including all dimensions ultimately as a unified whole.

Non-physical: The aspect of reality which is incorporeal, essential and supernatural. It does not display particle like properties, is not restricted to expression in the third dimension, and often exists in a state of potential.

Oneness: The quality of all separate parts being united as one, a state which is experienced only once a person is able to free themselves from mental interpretations such as identity. It is the underlying truth of this universe we live in.

Out-Of-Body Experience: The shifting of perception or point of view from that of physical reality, where one is restricted to a body, to a non-physical reality where one is not restricted to the physical existence which is experienced through a body. This transition usually gives one the perception of leaving one's body and one's bodily sensations behind. Hospital operating rooms are famous for this kind of experience. Often after returning from an out of body experience, a person who had lost consciousness can recollect information which by current scientific understanding they should have no way of knowing.

Physical: The aspect of reality which Pertains to substance or material made up of energy displaying particle like properties within the third dimension, that which involves the body as distinguished from the mind or spirit and is perceivable by the traditional senses.

Psychic: Of or pertaining to extrasensory information or abilities. Someone who is said to be "psychic" is a person who is skilled in the art and ability of extra sensory perception.

Reincarnation: A concept that energy (some may even say a soul) manifests and de manifests, embodying new forms. This thought gives rise to a belief that energy is the only constant and that lives come and go. It is a key ingredient to the concept of past lives.

Seer: A person who exhibits extrasensory abilities, which manifest most often in the form of clairvoyance who like a visionary, has unusual powers of foresight and unlimited access to universal truths. In some cultures, a seer is known as a prophet.

Spirit Guide: A true projection of Source into a thought form for a specific purpose. People become an energetic match to guides who are masters in the lessons, abilities, and problems that they are engaged in. They aid our growth. These entities gain and "learn" from the experience of this state of being as well. Their evolution is best served from a format that is not expressed in the physical which is why they chose to project into thought form, but not physical form. Guides may choose to portray a "personality" and "life story" that the person they are guiding relates to. Often guides offer a projection in the form of an image of themselves from a past life.

Spiritual Catalyst: A spiritual catalyst is a person who precipitates an event or a change in other people on the level of spirit.

Soul: The energetic, immaterial aspect of a living thing which is constant as it takes on different embodiments. Though a soul seems in and of its self a "thing," it is instead an essence. It is conscious energy.

Source: An alternative word for "God." A word used to represent the omnipresent, Omni benevolence within the universe. A word which signifies ultimate oneness, the united energy that makes up all that is.

Thought Form: Any thought, which has enough inherent energy that it becomes a configuration, shape or visual appearance and may manifest in a non-static way. There are traditionally three types of thought forms: 1) Energy which takes the image of the thinker, 2) Energy which takes the image of a material object and 3), Energy which takes a form entirely its own, expressing its qualities in the matter which it draws round it.

Transformation: A profound positive change in energetic vibration causing the physical reality to then inevitably change as well. A transformation is usually the product of increased awareness in which one consciously and deliberately brings about the alteration within themselves. Transformation can happen on the level of the individual or on a much larger scale, globally for example.

Tulpa: A commonly used name for a thought from.

ABOUT THE AUTHOR

Teal was born in Santa Fe New Mexico in the year 1984.

In the first years of her life, it became apparent that she had been born with extrasensory abilities. Among these abilities she was born with were clairvoyance, clairsentience, clairaudience, the ability to manipulate electromagnetic fields and the ability to communicate with thought forms. As she grew, unlike many children born with extrasensory abilities, her gifts did not go away. Her parents who were both Wilderness Rangers later accepted a job in the Wasatch-Cache National Forest of Utah, not knowing at the time about the intensely religious climate of the location. Word of her abilities got out very quickly and were not only frowned upon, but feared by many in the religious community. It was because of Teal's extrasensory abilities that she was inducted as a child, unbeknownst to her parents, into a local cult by a family acquaintance and was ritualistically tortured for thirteen years. She managed to escape from the cult when she was 19 years old. Since then, Teal has become a "spiritual catalyst" both accepting and utilizing her abilities to remind people of the united, energetic, nature of this universe and to teach people how to find bliss in the midst of even the most extreme circumstances.

CPSIA information can be obtained
at www.ICGtesting.com
Printed in the USA
LVHW08s1247210718
584520LV00001B/17/P